LIBRARY CONVERSATIONS

LIBRARY CONVERSATIONS

RECLAIMING INTERPERSONAL COMMUNICATION THEORY FOR UNDERSTANDING PROFESSIONAL ENCOUNTERS

MARIE L. RADFORD AND **GARY P. RADFORD**

An imprint of the American Library Association

CHICAGO 2017

ISBN: 978-0-8389-1484-7 (paper)

Library of Congress Cataloging-in-Publication Data

Names: Radford, Marie L., author. | Radford, Gary P., 1961- author.
Title: Library conversations : reclaiming interpersonal communication theory for understanding professional encounters / Marie L. Radford, Gary P. Radford.
Description: Chicago : ALA Neal-Schuman, an imprint of the American Library Association, 2017. | Includes bibliographical references and index.
Identifiers: LCCN 2016021764 | ISBN 9780838914847 (pbk. : alk. paper)
Subjects: LCSH: Communication in library science. | Interpersonal communication. | Librarians—Professional relationships. | Reference services (Libraries)
Classification: LCC Z665 .R25 2016 | DDC 020.1/4—dc23 LC record available at https://lccn .loc.gov/2016021764

Cover design by T.J. Johnson. Cover image: Perkins Library Reference Desk, 1970s (Duke University Archives). Text composition by Alejandra Diaz in the Charis SIL and Proxima Nova typefaces.

♾ This paper meets the requirements of ANSI/NISO Z39.48–1992 (Permanence of Paper).
Printed in the United States of America

21 20 19 18 17   5 4 3 2 1

In loving memory of
CHARLES HEIN JR.
ELSIE AND HOWARD RADFORD

CONTENTS

PART 1   RECLAIMING THEORY FOR LIBRARY CONTEXTS

ILLUSTRATIONS

PREFACE

This book is intended to be used by library professionals, students, and researchers interested in interpersonal communication in all types of libraries. It is organized into two parts. The first part, Reclaiming Theory for Library Contexts, includes chapters 1 through 4, which describe and discuss a number of theoretical frameworks for understanding interpersonal communication from Aristotle through John Locke, Jurgen Ruesch and Gregory Bateson, Paul Watzlawick and his colleagues, and Erving Goffman. These frameworks enable us to reclaim principles of communication for the Library and Information Science discipline. This part takes a broad approach, discussing basic principles and illustrating these with examples from different types of library interpersonal encounters, including those with colleagues, the public, managers, and subordinates.

Building on these theoretical foundations, in part two, Applying Theory to Reference Encounters, chapters 5 through 7 extend the discussions of the initial chapters and focus in on a specific type of library communication context, the reference encounter. Chapter 6 introduces a Content/Relational Model of Success in Reference Encounters, and liberally illustrates its components with examples from librarians and library users. This model not only rests on a strong theoretical base, but also is informed by a large amount of empirical research gathered by the authors and their colleagues over several decades.

We invite the reader to join with us in an effort to understand interpersonal encounters in libraries, which is certainly an important and worthy effort. We realize that there are no absolutes in anything to do with human communication. However, we firmly believe that you will greatly benefit from reading our book with an open mind, and from applying the insights provided here to your daily communication practice.

—*Marie L. Radford and Gary P. Radford*

ACKNOWLEDGMENTS

This book represents the culmination of research and writing that spans several decades. It is not possible to complete a book like this without a great deal of help. We first thank the Institute of Museum and Library Services; OCLC; and Rutgers, the State University of New Jersey, for funding and partnering on two large grant projects: *Seeking Synchronicity: Evaluating Virtual Reference Services from User, Non-User, and Librarian Perspectives,* and *Cyber Synergy: Seeking Sustainability through Collaboration between Virtual Reference and Social Q&A Sites,* which provided us with the opportunity to collect a large amount of data during the years 2005 to 2014. The findings from these projects inform this book and provided impetus for building the theoretical model that is described here.

We thank our colleagues who have actively engaged and collaborated with Marie on these two large grant projects. First among these is Lynn Silipigni Connaway, Senior Research Scientist at OCLC, who has become a close friend, as well as a valued collaborator and confidant for the well over a decade that she and Marie have worked together as co-principal investigators. Her contribution began in 2004 when she invited Marie to submit a grant proposal to IMLS, which was funded as the *Seeking Synchronicity* project. Her creativity, intelligence, and research expertise have been critically important to the gathering of the enormous amount of empirical data, analysis, and interpretation that underpins this book. She has generously given her permission to use examples from interviews, surveys, and transcripts originating in our grant-funded work and, along with OCLC, permission to feature the updated theoretical model that has been under construction since 2008, which makes its debut in an updated format within these pages.

Additionally, we would like to thank Jocelyn DeAngelis of Western New England University, whose work as project manager of the *Seeking Synchronicity* grant and whose collaboration, including her dissertation-related research on face-work and face threat in virtual environments, made a significant contribution to this book. We also recognize the contributions of Chirag Shah. of Rutgers University, who joined with Lynn and Marie in 2011 as a co-principal investigator on the *Cyber Synergy* project, and brought his expertise in collaborative information seeking into the mix. We also express our appreciation to the numerous anonymous librarians and users of libraries, virtual reference, and social question and answer services, who were willing to participate in the grant projects, lending their voices and expertise.

Editing and citation management assistance has also been critically important to this book, and we would especially like to thank three PhD students at Rutgers University. Appreciation and kudos are extended to Stefani Gomez for her editing expertise and for suggesting several examples used throughout the book. Also, we thank Stephanie Mikitish for being the resident NVivo expert for the duration of this book project, especially for wrangling transcript, interview, and survey examples. Another valuable contribution was made by Frank Bridges, whose expertise in graphic design was instrumental in helping Marie and Lynn to envision the theoretical model. A master's student from Rutgers University, Matt Bridgeman, is also recognized for his help with editing and citation management during our first phase of writing. We wish to thank Charles Harmon, now of Rowman and Littlefield, who contributed to this work while he was our editor at Neal-Schuman during the initial phase of this book's inception.

We also want to thank Rachel Chance and the editorial team at ALA Editions, including Angela Gwizdala and Helayne Beavers for guiding the book to completion, and for their enthusiasm and support in the final stages of editing, publication, and design. This book truly was an enormous undertaking that took several years to create. We are grateful to all and believe that without the individual and collective contributions of everyone mentioned above, this work would not have been possible.

PART 1

Reclaiming Theory for Library Contexts

Interpersonal Communication as Practical Wisdom

Reclaiming Aristotle's *Nicomachean Ethics* for the Professional Sphere

We feel that even if all possible scientific questions be answered, the problems of life have still not been touched at all.

—LUDWIG WITTGENSTEIN (1951)

THE IMPORTANCE OF A FOCUS ON INTERPERSONAL COMMUNICATION FOR LIBRARIANS AND INFORMATION PROFESSIONALS

How important is interpersonal communication in the work of librarians and other information professionals? Jaime LaRue, former director of the Douglas County Libraries in Colorado, asserted that communication is paramount for service excellence:

> In the years since I got my library degree, I have seen many service transactions. The ones that were best, that left patrons with the sense that they had been well-served, were not necessarily ones in which the right answer was given, but were interactions in which staff and patron connected, occupied the same mental and emotional space. The skill that matters most in reference is communication. Some of this can be taught, eye contact, open posture, smiling, and modulation of voice. Some of it, perhaps, cannot, or not as easily: the willingness to be open to another human being, to be fully present. (LaRue 2010, 28)

Here LaRue is referring to reference service in public libraries, but what he has to say can be generalized to an array of interactions at other types of libraries. The importance of being "fully present" in face-to-face (FtF) and virtual communication in the complex, challenging, and rapidly changing work environment of twenty-first-century libraries cannot be overstated. Whether you work in an academic, public, school, or special library, or other information environment, it is no surprise to find that the major part of your day is filled with frequent FtF and virtual interactions. A quick glance at advertisements for available library positions reveals that most list "excellent oral and written communication skills" among desired qualifications. Building positive relationships with library users, as well as changing managerial models that work towards more collegial teamwork and project-management approaches, has become a strategic direction for our organizations. The ability to engage in clear, nonconfrontational, and productive communication is increasingly critical to a library's success and to every individual's career potential.

This trend toward more emphasis on interpersonal communication in libraries is reflected in the educational and business world, where the desire to recruit employees who are skilled and comfortable communicators is well documented (Adams 2014; Bloomberg 2015). However, it is noteworthy that most books addressing "managerial communication" typically focus on the written aspects of communication. For example, in Guffey and Loewy's (2014) textbook on business communication, two-thirds of the chapters are devoted to written communication (e.g., memos, e-mail messages, positive letters, persuasive messages, formal and informal reports, "digital writing," and proposal writing). The chapters addressing oral communication are limited to a few very specific communication situations, such as giving presentations, conducting interviews, and communicating with people from different cultures. Similarly, in the library literature, an outstanding handbook, *Communicating Professionally, Third Edition,* by Ross and Nilsen (2013), also places its major emphasis on a limited range of communication skills (oral and written, including presentation skills and training others).

This book takes as its focus the domain of interpersonal communication in the library context. The term "interpersonal communication" refers specifically to those situations in which people communicate one-on-one in the context of a conversation. Examples of conversations in professional situations include reference and other service encounters with the public; collegial interactions among staff; and managerial encounters with staff, administrators, vendors, and funders. Conversations typically take place in FtF settings, but increasingly professional conversations occur in virtual environments such as e-mail, live chat, instant messaging (IM) services, text messaging, and in social networking sites such as Facebook and Twitter. This book will also consider interpersonal communication in these domains.

RECLAIMING INTERPERSONAL COMMUNICATION THEORY FOR LIBRARY AND INFORMATION SCIENCE

An ongoing concern for Library and Information Science (LIS) has been the need to move the field toward more theoretical richness and depth, and to explore and embrace the insights of academic disciplines beyond LIS, such as psychology, sociology, critical theory, and even philosophy (e.g., see Cibangu 2013; McKechnie and Pettigrew 2002; Radford 1993; Wiegand 1999). One objective of this book is to advance this movement with respect to theories developed in the academic realm of Communication Studies, and, in particular, their treatment of interaction in both FtF and virtual environments. Particular emphasis will be given to the relational theory of interpersonal communication articulated in the germinal theoretical work in human communication and psychology by Watzlawick, Beavin Bavelas, and Jackson (1967); Ruesch and Bateson (1968); and, in sociology, by Goffman (1967). The end result will be a fresh and insightful look at communication issues and problems that face librarians and other information professionals in their working lives.

One might ask why theories published in 1968 and 1967 will be relevant to a world in the second decade of the twenty-first century, which is being increasingly dominated by concerns dealing with electronically mediated communication on both the public and personal levels. In reply, we argue that it is the contemporary concern with technology, and its emphasis on the transmission of information, which must be transcended, and theories that consider communication in its human context need to be reclaimed. The fact that Gregory Bateson, Jurgen Ruesch, Paul Watzlawick, and Erving Goffman were writing in a time when the ubiquity of computers, the Internet, mobile technology, cell phones, and social media had yet to be imagined enables issues and problems in interpersonal communication to be considered more clearly. One problem when thinking about conceptions of communication within the theory and practice of LIS is that this discourse is dominated by issues concerning the transmission and delivery of content, rather than the communication processes that make such delivery possible and successful (or unsuccessful). This book will not address the technological means of transmission, that is, how a message, a piece of information, or an answer to a reference question can physically travel from a provider to a library client, or from colleague to colleague, in the most efficient manner possible. Rather, its focus will be on human conversations, which take place between people in each other's physical, or sometimes virtual, presence. In these encounters, information needs or queries are expressed, discussed, negotiated, and ultimately fulfilled (or not), and relationships are established and/or developed (or not).

The germinal relational theories developed in the 1950s and 1960s address precisely and clearly the *human* aspects of communication: Who are the people involved? Why are they speaking to each other? What relationship do they have with each other? How does each person feel about the other, and about herself? Do these people feel comfortable in each other's presence? Are they confident, happy, scared, intimidated, bored, or excited? What is it about the conversation that would make them feel this way? Where is the conversation taking place? Why is it taking place? What is at stake for the participants in the conversation? Who holds power in this conversation, and how does this shape the conversation? What is it about the conversation that enables the participants to interact at all, and the conversation to proceed smoothly? These questions represent the human context of conversation in which all of our encounters with one another, whether social or professional (or a blend of both), take place.

With a few exceptions, questions such as these are either ignored or given short shrift in contemporary treatments of communication within LIS. This book aims to bring a different focus to the ways one conceptualizes the above questions, and push thought beyond the trite or expected answers, to provide a reenvisioned and deep conceptualization of in-person and virtual communication in library settings.

THE TWO FACES OF INTERPERSONAL COMMUNICATION

Our consideration of interpersonal communication begins with the observation that conversation with others is an activity that seemingly has two distinct faces. On the one hand, interacting with others seems so easy. We talk to our friends, family members, colleagues, and even the person at the convenience store, and at no time do we feel compelled to reflect on what is happening. Talking to others is a mundane part of everyday life and, for the most part, everyone around us, even a small child, seems particularly competent to do it. Every day we find ourselves in interpersonal communication situations. We chat, consult, gossip, bicker, argue, compliment, request, and so on. Virtually, we text, e-mail, chat, and tweet fluidly throughout our day. We certainly do not feel the need to be experts in communication theory to be able to successfully engage in a conversation with another person via any mode we choose.

On the other hand, interpersonal communication can sometimes be very difficult. We find ourselves faced with situations where we are required to interact with another person, but we are not sure what to do or say, or we are sensitive to the possible reactions of the other person, or acutely aware of the consequences of the interaction. Consider the situation where a person must summon up all of his courage to ask someone he has secretly admired to go out to dinner, or a situation in which when someone is unsure what to say to a recently bereaved person, or the fateful interaction when someone asks for a partner's hand in marriage. To apply this to the professional context in the library, consider times when a new librarian wants to speak up in a staff meeting, but is afraid that his input will be unwelcome, when a library director needs to confront an employee about chronic lateness, when we receive an upsetting e-mail or text from a colleague, when a library user insists that an overdue fine has been paid, although the computer indicates it is still outstanding, or when a university student is talking loudly on a cell phone while at the service desk. We can all certainly think of times when communication becomes stressful and risky. In situations such as these, we are often afraid we will inadvertently react the wrong way, and we would be grateful for some theory or advice to draw upon in knowing what to do and what to say.

In the professional context, we can agree that interpersonal communication situations fall along a continuum from easy (requiring little or no reflection) to difficult (requiring reflection and planning). Speaking to colleagues in the break room or sending a quick e-mail about scheduling a routine meeting would require less reflection than presenting a budget request at a board meeting, giving an annual performance review to a subordinate, or responding to a nasty phone message left by an irate library client. The question we must address is: What is it about these latter conversations that make them seem difficult and require more thought and reflection?

There are important ways in which interpersonal communication in a professional context is different from casual social conversation. For example, there are often tangible outcomes to a professional conversation. A potential promotion may be on the line, the fate of your proposal for a project or program, a large gift from a potential library donor, or a new departmental assignment. Also, the success of a particular interaction may not just reflect on you personally, but also on the group of people with whom you work, or even the organization that you represent. Explaining a poor performance evaluation to a subordinate is not only a conversation that transmits information; it may lead to that person being fired from the organization, low morale in the department, or a potentially rocky relationship with that person (and her allies) in the future.

INTERPERSONAL COMMUNICATION
AS A STRATEGIC ACTIVITY

This book considers interpersonal communication in professional situations. However, this is done in a way that challenges dominant understandings of what constitutes "successful" interpersonal communication. Far and away the most common way to view work-related interpersonal communication is to see it as a kind of strategy in which a professional uses conversation as a means to achieve particular ends, such as: How do I get employees to respond to my commands? How do I gain their respect? How do I increase morale? David Berlo, writing in 1960, offers a view that still resonates today: "Given a purpose for communicating, a response which is to be elicited, a communicator hopes that his [sic] communication will have fidelity. By fidelity, we mean that he [sic] will get what he [sic] wants" (1960, 40). The focus of strategic interpersonal communication is the goal the communicator wishes to achieve through engaging in a conversation. For example, consider the conversations that might take place at a library conference or professional meeting. Someone attending such an event might ask: What is the best way to conduct a conversation so that the person will consider hiring me for a job opening she has for an associate director, or help me with advice for a project or large ticket item purchase, or give me access to a high-level committee appointment?

In these situations, we are often acutely aware of not only *what* we have to say, but also the *way* we choose to say it. During a difficult or high-stakes professional interpersonal communication situation, we become much more self-aware of our communication behaviors and whether they are correct and appropriate. Consider the feelings you have anticipating a job interview, giving a public presentation, preparing for an information literacy instruction session or adult-services program, or participating in a brainstorming or problem-solving group of library leaders. We become intensely conscious that *how we act* is as important as *what we say*. We want to *look* informed; we want to *appear* professional, confident, and knowledgeable to the other person or group. Everything, including our words and nonverbal behaviors, is vitally important in how meaning is constructed by ourselves and others.

So, right away, we are mindful that there are two parts to interpersonal communication: *what we say* and *how we say it.* The goal for the professional interpersonal communicator is to match these two aspects in order to achieve a desired outcome. This viewpoint has spawned a huge industry of books and workshops that purport to help professional communicators do just that. In this industry, the alignment of what is said with how it is said is reduced to a series of tips and tactics made famous by Dale Carnegie, who referred to such matching as "human engineering." Carnegie writes: "about 15 percent of one's financial success is due to one's technical knowledge and about 85 percent is due to skill in human engineering—to personality and the ability to lead people" (1937, xiv). Carnegie's conception of communication as "human engineering" reflects a common belief in the power of communication—the belief that the right communication techniques can predict and control the behavior of others in systematic and beneficial ways. Best-selling library management textbooks (e.g., see Moran, Stueart, and Morner 2012) typically present a "best practices" approach to communication that reinforces these instrumental and strategic conceptions of communication; that is, the view that communication is an instrument or tool for achieving particular ends. Such texts may provide lists of "what to do" and "what not to do" to communicate effectively, which usually means that communication encounters for managers are presented as goal-directed events where the manager enters into a conversation, meets with a group, or sends an e-mail in order to forward a particular goal (e.g., to inquire about progress on a project, or to request information, feedback, or action).

However, this is not the path taken in this book. We believe that successful, effective communication is more about building relationships than merely persuasion or getting others to do what we want them to do. Reflect for a moment on what the world would be like if Carnegie's concept of human engineering were true. Our conversations would be very different. For one thing, we would be continually aware of our own attempts to engineer the responses of others, and we would lose the spontaneity, unpredictability, and creativity of normal conversational life. We would also be acutely aware of the attempts of others to control our perceptions and behavior because they also have their own professional and personal goals in mind. But even a cursory reflection on the nature of our own interpersonal communication activities, whether in a social or professional setting, reveals that the majority of our conversations are not driven by such cynical motives. In fact, the people who do try to manipulate others through conversations are recognized very quickly. They come across as phony, cold, and insincere. The act of trying to manipulate others through conversational tactics and strategies may backfire, leading to more resistance than compliance.

Here's a more detailed library-related example. Mike, the newly elected president of a small, specialized library association, has discovered that the association has no planning document in place. He decides his goal for his presidential year will be to pursue the development of a three-to-five-year strategic plan. His plan of action is to hold a one-day retreat that would result in the creation of draft goals and objectives, perhaps with some target dates. He talks about his idea to his vice-president, Maria, who is enthusiastic, and the two of them then approach several consultants to get some pricing ideas for holding a retreat for the full Executive Board (EB). With what they consider to be some reasonably priced proposals in hand, they bring up this idea and plan of action at the next EB meeting. Mike prepares a short presentation and fully expects it to go well. He pictures the EB enthusiastically accepting his proposal so he can move ahead, prepare a contract for the selected consultant, and schedule the retreat.

However, Mike and Maria are stunned when the EB pushes back against their idea by saying that "groundwork needs to be done first," and that "treasury dollars are better spent in member benefits rather than on developing strategic plans," which they consider to be useless. One influential member states (in a dramatic tone of voice): "In my experience, strategic plans are a waste of everyone's time and money and wind up lining the bottom of drawers." Others smile and nod their head vigorously in agreement. Mike and Maria are deflated and upset. It is apparent to them that their idea is a good one, and they find it hard to believe that others do not share this vision.

In their discussion following the meeting, Mike and Maria try to figure out what went wrong. Did they not fully explain the reasons behind the need for a strategic plan? What should they have done to lobby members before the meeting? What can be done now to change people's minds? It is apparent that despite their strategic groundwork of talking to consultants, obtaining proposals, and preparing a persuasive presentation, they were not prepared for the pushback and oppositional points made by the members, and for the discouraging and resounding defeat. They are at a loss to explain what went wrong with their carefully crafted proposal and presentation. Clearly, Mike and Maria, despite their best efforts, have not been able to control the transmission of their ideas or to manipulate the EB to accept their suggested plan of action.

Indeed, the example above, as well as our everyday experience, tells us that we do not have the means to directly control the perceptions and conduct of others through conversation. We can certainly try, and we may convince ourselves that the behavior of another is the direct result of our conversational style, but more often than not the impression we inadvertently give is of trying to control communication in order to control others. We can fake sympathy, overtly gesture in our speeches, smile and gaze into another's eyes, or e-mail an apology that should be given FtF, and so forth, but it does not take a great deal of sensitivity for others to recognize what is going on in these insincere ploys.

So why do we continue to believe that conversations can be used in a strategic manner? Despite the experience of our own interpersonal communication activities, many of us remain compelled by the belief that the ability to control what we say and how we say it in some systematic and perhaps theoretically informed manner is a kind of Holy Grail that will enable us to control others so that they behave in particular ways. Perhaps we buy books with titles like *Library Conversations: Reclaiming Interpersonal Communication Theory for Understanding Professional Encounters* with the hope that within these pages we will find that ultimate collection of tips and tactics that will enable us to achieve our professional goals when dealing with others. Some people reading this book or taking a course or workshop in communication would claim that their motive is to improve their personal communication skills, and there are plenty of communication scholars and practitioners who are ready and willing to respond to this perceived need. They make careers out of identifying communication problems in many kinds of areas, including personal relationships, small groups, organizations, and so on. Consumers of this communication advice see the main function of communication teachers as being able to offer solutions, strategies, or even theories to help to deal with the various communication problems they have identified.

The problem is that this means-ends approach to professional communication is not particularly effective or useful, despite its superficial appeal. We can only wish interpersonal communication worked this way. If strictly instrumental and strategic approaches to communication were successful, then professional conversations would not be considered so difficult. All you would have to do is look up the appropriate tips and tactics in the *Handbook of Strategic Communication* and carry them out as directed to reach the desired outcome. However, it seems that no matter how many books on professional communication we read or workshops we take, the problems of interpersonal communication remain with us. We still feel nervous giving a formal presentation; we still act awkwardly when giving constructive feedback or discussing a poor evaluation with a staff member; we labor over the wording of an e-mail or text message; we do not know how to respond to a chat reference user who becomes irate and impatient; we feel ill at ease trying to make connections at a library conference or professional networking event. Even with tips and tactics in hand, the conversations or threads never seem to go exactly the way we would like, and other people never seem to react in exactly the way we would like or expect them to react. Sometimes what we do inadvertently leads to problems and issues that would not have arisen if this particular conversation had not taken place, or if we had not pushed the send button on an e-mail.

Perhaps Austrian philosopher Ludwig Wittgenstein captured this feeling best when he wrote: "We feel that even if *all possible* scientific questions be answered, the problems of life have still not been touched at all" (Wittgenstein 1951, 187). The same might be said of our understanding of interpersonal communication. Despite our arsenal of tips, tactics, and strategies, the next conversation we have seems to have a life of its own. Imagine that social scientists and communication scholars had achieved a perfect scientific understanding of interpersonal communication. Imagine that they now know exactly how conversations work and why people behave the way they do when they communicate. Even then, the "problems of life," our communication in real situations, would remain as problematic as ever. As we shall see, *knowing* is not the same as *doing*. With interpersonal communication, it is not what you *know*, but what you *do* that is important. This book offers a compelling explanation of why this is so, and beyond this, how you can develop a deeper understanding of the communication process, as well as a new perspective for guiding your own interpersonal encounters. As we shall discuss in the following section, the idea of placing the emphasis on what we do, rather than on the knowledge we have, is by no means new.

INTERPERSONAL COMMUNICATION AS PRACTICAL WISDOM

The Greek philosopher Aristotle addressed the distinction between knowing and doing, and its importance for human conduct, over 2,300 years ago in his *Nicomachean Ethics* (Aristotle 2004). His distinction remains instructive in articulating a realistic and useful view of interpersonal communication in the present and beyond. The key to Aristotle's observations is his differentiation between "scientific knowledge" and "practical wisdom." This distinction hinges on the notion of variance, or change. Aristotle proposed that the rational soul consists of two parts: "one with which we contemplate those things whose first principles are invariable, and one with which we contemplate things which are variable" (Aristotle 2004, 145). Aristotle wants us to understand that there are certain things in the universe that are unchanging, and will not change regardless of how much we speculate on them or wish they would. An example of something Aristotle considers invariable are the principles of geometry. We can sit and contemplate the judgment that "the sum of the angles of a triangle is or is not equal to two right angles" (Aristotle 2004, 151) all we want, but the principle that "the sum of the angles of a triangle is equal to two right angles" (i.e., the sum of the angles of a triangle is always 180 degrees, and the sum of two right angles—90 degrees plus 90 degrees—is also always equal to 180 degrees) is invariable. The principle does not change simply because we choose to think about it differently. Knowledge about things that are invariable is considered by Aristotle to be "scientific."

Scientific knowledge deals with principles that are true by necessity. Such knowledge is considered eternal "because everything that is of necessity in the unqualified sense is eternal; and what is eternal cannot come into being or cease to be" (Aristotle 2004, 148). When the sun finally blows up and destroys the earth, the principle that "the sum of the angles of a triangle is equal to two right angles" will continue to be the case. The principle is eternal. It cannot "come into being" and it cannot "cease to be." It has always been so, and it will always be so. Because of its necessary and eternal nature, it makes no sense to deliberate about scientific knowledge. It cannot be questioned or changed. The eternal principles of scientific knowledge can only be discovered and then demonstrated. So we can demonstrate the principle that "the sum of the angles of a triangle is equal to two right angles" through a logical proof, and we can use this principle to demonstrate other principles that logically follow from it. But it is pointless to contemplate, for example, the existence of a triangle whose angles add up to more than 180 degrees, or posit a triangle with four sides.

A scientific approach to interpersonal communication, in Aristotle's sense of the term, attempts to discover and articulate the invariable and necessary principles underlying all particular acts of communication. There is such a principle, which was articulated by information scientist Claude E. Shannon in 1949: "The fundamental problem of communication is that of reproducing at one point either exactly or approximately a message selected at another point" (Shannon 1949, 31). No matter which specific example of communication we might think of—for example, delivering a speech, making a phone call, sending an e-mail, talking to a friend, watching television, or writing a blog or tweet—all of these instances require, by necessity, that they realize a case of "reproducing at one point either exactly or approximately a message selected at another point," or else they could not be considered examples of communication. The actual instances (or modes) of communication may vary and change, but the underlying principle remains unchanged and eternal. Shannon's great contribution to communication research and theory in the twentieth century was that he was able to articulate this principle precisely and rigorously using mathematical theorems. He was able to establish abstract and generalizable laws that would hold true for any particular case of communication, whether it is sending signals down a telephone line to having a conversation with your best friend. As Campbell notes, "In spite of the fact that the theorems of information theory were intended chiefly for radio and telephone engineers, they can be used to investigate *any* system in which a 'message' is sent from one place to another" (Campbell 1982, 17) and further, that "just as Newton's laws of motion are not restricted to particular sorts of motion by special kinds of bodies, Shannon's laws of information are universal" (Campbell 1982, 17).

This is a very attractive way of approaching conceptualizations of communication. It holds out the promise that we are dealing with something profoundly real and true, an eternal principle that remains unchanging behind a range of diverse and changing appearances. Warren Weaver famously wrote that a principle like this is "so general that one does not need to say what kinds of symbols are being considered—whether written letters or words, or musical notes, or spoken words, or symphonic music, or pictures. The theory is deep enough so that the relationships it reveals indiscriminately apply to all these and to other forms of communication." Weaver continues: "This means, of course, that the theory is sufficiently imaginatively motivated so that it is dealing with the real inner core of the communication problem—with those basic relationships which hold in general, no matter what special form the actual case may take" (Weaver 1949, 25). It should come as no surprise, therefore, that a scientific approach is a very powerful force in our attempts to describe and understand communication, including interpersonal communication.

However, as Aristotle pointed out over two thousand years ago, describing a phenomenon such as communication in terms of unchanging and eternal principles does not necessarily help us in our day-to-day activities or with the "problems of life," as Wittgenstein put it. Even if we could describe the transmission of information from a sender to a receiver in rigorous mathematical terms (see Shannon and Weaver 1949), how does that knowledge help navigate a tricky conversation with an employee? For example, Angela, a library department head, is about to engage in a highly stressful performance appraisal meeting with an employee, Noah, who is belligerent at times and is performing below expectations. How does knowing about the unchanging and eternal principles of information transfer help her in this situation? The simple answer is that it does not help at all. Interpersonal communication needs to be described and understood in the context of real life. It requires what Aristotle called "practical wisdom" or "phronesis."

Aristotle wrote that practical wisdom "is not concerned with universals only; it must also take cognizance of particulars, because it is concerned with particulars, and conduct has its sphere in particular circumstances" (2004, 154). For example, let us return to our manager Angela, who is facing a difficult performance appraisal interview. She is faced with a particular person, a particular problem, and a particular set of circumstances. Ideally, Angela, in her managerial role, wishes to encourage and help Noah to improve his performance. If not, she may be faced with the unpleasant duty of sanctioning him, engaging in a long course of documentation and review, or worse, eventually laying him off. Angela may well seek out tips and tactics from a book with a title like *How to Conduct an Employee Appraisal Interview.* However, in the final analysis, she realizes that the generalized advice (scientific principles) given in the book will only get her so far. The situation and conversation Angela faces are not generalized, but are unique. The problem employee, Noah, is a unique person who does not appear in any communication self-help book. He has a unique personal history and a unique set of attitudes, emotions, and expectations. He also has a unique relationship with Angela, in her role as his manager. As Aristotle has noted, in order to conduct a successful interview, Angela must be cognizant of the particulars of *this* person and *this* situation, which is happening at *this* time. What she requires is not knowledge, but practical wisdom; not the demonstration of eternal truths, but the ability to adapt to a dynamic set of unique circumstances. The question she needs to address is not, "what do *I know* about communication?" (scientific knowledge), but rather "what should *I do* in this conversation?" (practical wisdom).

Practical wisdom is gained from life experience rather than formal instruction or education. It is acquired over time, through trial and error, and through experience. As such, it is not gained easily. As Aristotle observes, "Although the young develop ability in geometry and mathematics and become wise in such matters, they are not thought to develop prudence. The reason for this is that prudence also involves knowledge of particular facts, which become known from experience; and [the young are] not experienced, because experience takes some time to acquire" (Aristotle 2004, 155–56). People learn what works and what does not, and the results of these lessons can be carried over into future life experiences. If you have previously had the experience of meeting with a problematic person or two and giving them a less-than-stellar performance review, this reflection on your own experience can be much more valuable than consulting a rule book of dos and don'ts. The question of how you answer the question, "what should I do?" for yourself in every unique interpersonal situation you encounter lies at the heart of a practical and pragmatic approach to interpersonal communication that will form the theoretical underpinnings of this book.

We should stress that when we use the term "theory" here, we are not addressing formal academic theories of the kind that would be found in a communication textbook such as the one by Stephen Littlejohn and Karen Foss (2010). Neither are we are looking to articulate another theory of communication to add to Littlejohn and Foss's list. Rather we are concerned with the theories of communication that people use in their everyday and professional lives as librarians or library staff members to help make sense of particular communication situations that guide their behavior in those situations. We want to offer a practical way (in Aristotle's sense) of conceptualizing interpersonal communication that we think will be more useful than the dominant scientifically-motivated views that most people have, and which communication scholarship has promoted for its own particular ends. A practical view of communication theory helps people deal with questions such as: How do I know what to say to someone at a professional networking event? How do I deal with an embarrassing *faux pas* at a formal meeting? How do I approach my supervisor to ask for a raise or a promotion? How do I best help a frustrated student with a complex query in chat reference? As Aristotle pointed out, there is no single or correct answer to any of these questions, because each of these situations is unique and will require a consideration of the "sphere of particular circumstances" (Aristotle 2004, 154) that constitutes each one. So our first insight needs to be that a scientific theory of interpersonal communication is not going to be sufficient to address specific communication situations. The question specifically addressed in this book is: "What kind of theory do I need to bring to bear in order to successfully deal with unique interpersonal communication encounters in professional situations?" We recognize that people in professional situations have goals, and that they will utilize concepts of people and situations (theories) they believe will help them achieve those goals. We recognize that choices will be made and actions will be taken in response to what they believe interpersonal communication to be, and how it works. We believe relational and interactional theories (to be discussed in detail in the coming chapters) are more useful (practical) than others in making these choices. A scientific and mathematical account of information transmission may be a rigorous and scientific account of a very complex phenomenon, but it is not at all useful in helping people deal with FtF and virtual communication situations.

For example, to foreshadow the usefulness of the relational approach, we return to our scenario above with Angela and Noah. Imagine that if instead of waiting for the daunting personnel review, Angela had scheduled regular meetings with Noah upon recognizing his lagging performance. These regular meetings could be focused on specific areas that Angela wanted to address. Perhaps Noah was found to be engaged in "e-mail wars" with other staff members. Noah could be asked about his rationale and made aware that perhaps his reactions have become habitual. He could be debriefed and coached on how to respond to a provocative e-mail. Perhaps he was seen being aggressive when confronting difficult library users. When Angela observes this, she could intervene, model calm behavior, and then put a discussion centering on her guidance of, and expectations for, Noah's future behavior on the agenda for their next meeting. Angela's stance would be constructive and help Noah to learn from missteps while focusing on particular instances, rather than on "correcting belligerent behavior." Angela could then ask Noah to reflect on his experiences and learning over time. They can discuss successful, as well as unsuccessful, encounters he has had. Noah could be asked to set future agendas for their regular meetings. The annual personnel review will take on a different focus as their professional relationship gradually develops. Of course, this approach may not always go well, because Noah has to respond in a positive manner, but we already have discussed how difficult it is to take the opposite route of striving to control the behaviors of others. (There will be more discussion of this to come as the book unfolds.) It also takes time; however, it can be argued that the time spent building a positive relationship and coaching a staff member is much more productive than that used for documenting a strong case for dismissal. Our overarching goal is to provide a theoretical account based in practical wisdom, which will better enable information professionals to achieve their communication goals.

REFERENCES

Adams, Susan. 2014. "The 10 Skills Employers Most Want in 2015 Graduates." www.forbes.com/sites/susanadams/2014/11/12/the-10-skills-employers-most-want-in-2015-graduates/.

Aristotle. 2004. *The Nicomachean Ethics*. Translated by James Alexander Kerr Thomson, Hugh Tredennick, and Jonathan Barnes. New York: Penguin Books.

Berlo, David. K. 1960. *The Process of Communication: An Introduction to Theory and Practice*. New York: Holt, Rinehart and Winston.

Bloomberg, 2015. "Job Skills Companies Want but Can't Get." www.bloomberg.com/graphics/2015-job-skills-report/.

Campbell, Jeremy. 1982. *Grammatical Man: Information, Entropy, Language, and Life*. New York: Simon and Schuster.

Carnegie, Dale. 1937. *How to Win Friends and Influence People*. New York: Pocket Books.

Cibangu, Sylvain K. 2013. "A Memo of Qualitative Research for Information Science: Toward Theory Construction." *Journal of Documentation* 69 (2): 194–213.

Goffman, Erving. 1967. *Interaction Ritual: Essays on Face-to-Face Behavior*. Garden City, New York: Doubleday.

Guffey, Mary Ellen, and Dana Loewy. 2014. *Business Communication: Process and Product,* 8th edition. Stamford, CT: Cengage Learning.

LaRue, Jamie. 2010. "Theory Meets Practice: Educators and Directors Talk." In *Reference Renaissance: Current and Future Trends,* edited by Marie L. Radford and David R. Lankes, 28- 34. New York: Neal-Schuman.

Littlejohn, Stephen. W., and Karen A. Foss. 2010. *Theories of Human Communication.* 10th edition. Los Angeles: Wavelength Press, Inc.

McKechnie, Lynn M., and Karen E. Pettigrew. 2002. "Surveying the Use of Theory in Library and Information Science Research: A Disciplinary Perspective." *Library Trends* 50 (3), 506–517.

Moran, Barbara B., Robert D. Stueart, and Claudia J. Morner. 2012. *Library and Information Center Management,* 8th edition. Greenwood Village, CO: Libraries Unlimited.

Radford, Marie L. 1993. "Relational Aspects of Reference Interactions: A Qualitative Investigation of the Perceptions of Users and Librarians in the Academic Library." PhD diss., Rutgers, The State University of New Jersey.

Ross, Catherine S., and Kirsti Nilsen. 2013. *Communicating Professionally.* 3rd ed. New York: ALA Neal-Schuman.

Ruesch, Jurgen, and Gregory Bateson. 1968. *Communication: The Social Matrix of Psychiatry.* New York: W. W. Norton.

Shannon, Claude E. 1949. "The Mathematical Theory of Communication." In *The Mathematical Theory of Communication,* by Claude E. Shannon and Warren Weaver, 31 – 125. Urbana, IL: University of Illinois Press.

Watzlawick, Paul, Janet Beavin Bavelas, and Don D. Jackson. 1967. *Pragmatics of Human Communication.* New York: Norton.

Weaver, Warren. 1949. "Recent Contributions to the Mathematical Theory of Communication." In *The Mathematical Theory of Communication,* by Claude E. Shannon and Warren Weaver, 3–28. Urbana, IL: University of Illinois Press.

Wiegand, Wayne. A. 1999. "Tunnel Vision and Blind Spots: What the Past Tells Us about the Present; Reflections on the Twentieth-Century History of American Librarianship." *Library Quarterly* 69 (1), 1–32.

Wittgenstein, Ludwig. 1951. *Tractatus Logico-Philosophcus.* Translated by Charles K. Ogden. New York: Humanities Press.

2

Interpersonal Communication as Civil Communication

Reclaiming John Locke's *An Essay Concerning Human Understanding*

We have to cure ourselves of the itch for absolute knowledge and power. We have to close the distance between the push-button order and the human act. We have to touch people.

—JACOB BRONOWSKI (1973, 374)

The distinction between practical wisdom and scientific knowledge identified by Aristotle (2004) discussed in chapter 1 is crucial for an appropriate understanding of interpersonal communication for information professionals. The distinction is essential because often we either fail to recognize this distinction or, if we do recognize it, we privilege the scientific over the practical. We all can agree on the importance of making common-sense and practical decisions in everyday communication situations, yet we downplay that knowledge because we think scientific knowledge is somehow more prestigious, more real, more significant, or that it has been investigated and verified by experts who know much more about these things than we do. We believe that information in books by communication "experts" must be better than the knowledge we have acquired through our life experiences. We imagine people who read this book, and books like it, will be expecting to find something more akin to Aristotle's scientific knowledge—principles, strategies, theories, and so on—that tell us the truth about what happens when we communicate.

However, as Aristotle observed, practical common-sense knowledge is more useful than scientific knowledge for dealing with real problems in the day-to-day world. Intuitively, we all know this: "The sum of the angles of a triangle is equal to two right angles" may get you a good score on standardized tests such as the SATs or GREs, but it will not help much with everyday life problems. Aristotle wrote, "That is why some people who do not possess theoretical knowledge are more effective in action (especially if they are experienced) than others who do possess it" (2004, 154). When we downplay common-sense, practical wisdom, and privilege scientific accounts based on eternal and unchanging principles, we may get a distorted and potentially dysfunctional view of interpersonal communication as we attempt to navigate and manage our encounters. This chapter discusses how having scientific theories of interpersonal communication can actually hinder our attempts to communicate effectively in real-life situations. We then discuss an alternative theory, based in large part on Aristotle's concept of practical wisdom, and advocate that this is a much more useful path for library professionals to follow.

WHAT HAPPENS WHEN WE THINK ABOUT COMMUNICATION SCIENTIFICALLY? THE TRANSMISSION THEORY OF COMMUNICATION

Take a moment to reflect on your understanding of the term "communication." What kinds of things come to mind? Our confident prediction is that you will probably come up with a description that reflects Shannon's principle that "the fundamental problem of communication is that of reproducing at one point either exactly or approximately a message selected at another point" (Shannon 1949, 31). You might not say it exactly in the same way as Shannon, but it will probably be something very close. You might say something like, "communication is about the exchange of messages" or "it is about having your ideas understood by another person." If this is the case, you are articulating a version of the *transmission theory of communication.* You are thinking about communication as a process of moving a message from one place, person, or mind to another. If you did respond to our question in this manner, you would certainly not be alone in doing so. W. Barnett Pearce observed: "If you were to ask the first ten people you meet on the street to define 'communication,' all ten would likely give some version of what we call the transmission theory" (Pearce 1994, 18–19). Communication scholar James Carey argues that the transmission view is the most prevalent conception of communication in our culture, and perhaps in all industrialized cultures. Carey writes: "Our basic orientation to communication remains grounded, at the deepest roots of our thinking, in the idea of transmission" (Carey 1992, 15). Michael Reddy (1979) has noted our extensive use of the conduit metaphor in describing communicative acts. In this metaphor, "the speaker puts ideas (objects) into words (containers) and sends them (along a conduit) to a hearer who takes the idea/objects out of the word/containers" (Lakoff and Johnson 1980, 10). People have a sincere belief in the ontological existence of "ideas" in the "mind," in the physical process of transmission, whereby messages are physically transferred from one place to another. A commonly held conviction is that the brain processes and reproduces messages, that is, the brain somehow extracts the meaning from symbols to derive the ideas that are contained within them.

The principle that communication is the transmission of information from a sender to a receiver is so taken-for-granted in our culture that we do not even recognize it as a theory. Rather people see it as a description of something real and intrinsic to the world. Radford (1999, 1993) found that academic librarians held this view in discussing successful reference encounters. Librarians reported that the goal of these interactions was to transfer or deliver information about collections and searching strategies from themselves to students. If such information was not transmitted or delivered, then the reference encounter is often considered to be unsuccessful. An example of a misunderstanding or failure at the public library reference desk is provided by Chris Martin, Reference Librarian at the Allentown (Pennsylvania) Public Library. Martin notes

> I think it happens a lot when the librarian latches onto a keyword that's used in a very common question. So like, they hear the word "tax" and immediately shift into "we can't give tax advice as we are not tax professionals." Or to give a specific example that happened the other day, as a large public library, during tax season we get well over a hundred inquiries a day about our available tax forms. One day a patron approached our reference desk and asked for help "finding a form," at which point he was promptly and courteously directed to our tax table and informed that "all our forms are right there against the wall." He ventured off, only to return a few minutes later, clearly confused, and when asked if he found what he needed, let us know that he didn't see a rental agreement form anywhere on the table. (personal communication as told to Stefani Gomez)

Clearly, viewing this case in terms of a transmission model of communication can only lead to the conclusion that this particular interaction failed. The message sent did not equal the message received. If the reference librarian had not taken the question on face value, but instead had taken a few more moments and asked a follow-up question to really understand the person's request, the misunderstanding could have been avoided easily. But this follow-up would have required a *conversation* between the librarian and the library user, and, as we shall see, conversations are much more than simple cases of back-and-forth information transfer between two people.

The common belief in the reality of communication as a process of transmission conforms to and is confirmed by dictionary definitions of the term "communication." The *Oxford English Dictionary* (OED) (2015) defines the transmission sense of the term "communication" as follows: "The transmission or exchange of information, knowledge, or ideas, by means of speech, writing, mechanical or electronic media, etc." The metaphor underlying this definition is that of *movement;* communication is the means by which something (a message, an idea, or a piece of information) gets moved from one place to another. What is actually being moved, and why it is being moved, is secondary to the act of movement itself. Claude Shannon made this explicit in his mathematical model of communication: "Frequently the messages have a *meaning* . . . These semantic aspects of communication are irrelevant to the engineering problem" (Shannon 1949, 31). As we shall see, this emphasis on movement, rather than content, is a big liability when trying to understand and explain *interpersonal* communication as a process of transmission. In a conversation, *what is said, why the person is saying it,* and *how it is interpreted* are of much more significance than the simple fact that messages are moving back and forth.

THE TRANSMISSION THEORY AS IDEALIZATION: JOHN LOCKE'S "PHILOSOPHICAL COMMUNICATION"

The weakness of the transmission view to explain what happens in interpersonal communication encounters can be found in the very sources the OED provides. A key citation given is John Locke's ([1690] 1975) *An Essay Concerning Human Understanding.* The example from Locke cited by the OED (2015) is the sentence fragment: "to make Words serviceable to the end of Communication." The complete paragraph from which this sentence fragment is taken describes a view of communication that could have been uttered by any modern person some 320 years later:

> To make Words serviceable to the end of Communication, it is necessary
> . . . that they excite, in the Hearer, exactly the same Idea, they stand for
> in the Mind of the speaker. Without this, Men fill one another's Heads

with noise and sounds; but convey not thereby their Thoughts, and lay not before one another their Ideas, which is the end of Discourse and Language. (Locke [1690] 1975, 478)

As Locke uses the term, "communication" becomes the conduit for the exciting of ideas in the mind of a hearer that correspond to the ideas in the mind of a speaker. Locke's use of the term "excite," describes words "exciting" in the hearer the same idea as the idea in the mind of a speaker, is a physical metaphor that invokes the image of something like an electrical current passing between two points and a light being activated at the destination. Indeed, the often-seen image of the light bulb representing someone having an idea follows perfectly from this description.

Locke's transmission conception of communication, as referenced by the OED, makes intuitive sense to us today, but the key term in Locke's account that is often overlooked is the word "exactly," as in the sentence, "they [words] excite, in the Hearer, *exactly the same Idea,* they stand for in the Mind of the speaker" (italics added). We know from our everyday experience that it is virtually impossible to communicate what we have in our minds such that the person we are speaking to holds *exactly* the same idea after we express it to them. If that were true, understanding would be perfect; there would be no misunderstandings or ambiguity. How often can we say that has happened in our professional and everyday lives? With some reflection, you may be able to recall a recent miscommunication that surprised you when you thought you were perfectly "clear" in a request, explanation, or instruction.

For instance, the authors were told of this example:

> At our public library we keep a file with descriptions and contact information for all the clubs in the area. Maintaining this file is generally the responsibility of the newest hire and the head of reference informed our newest member, Susan, to begin on the club file. While she thought she was being perfectly clear that she wanted the new hire to keep the current file maintained, Susan interpreted the request to mean that she should start the file from scratch. The miscommunication was discovered weeks later when the website editor asked if the new club file should be added to the website. (personal communication, Stefani Gomez, May 13, 2015)

Here is a verbatim example from a Virtual Reference Service (VRS) live chat transcript[1] of a time when a user attempted to ask what she thought was a self-evident and clear question, but turned out to be one that resulted in a complex interaction. The encounter was frustrating to the user, as can be seen in the eventual abrupt ending with expletive deleted. While reading through this transcript, think about how imperfect our understanding is of what might be a simple request. The transcript displays a growing tension between librarian and user as the user attempts to elicit a desired answer, while the librarian is attempting to provide one. Neither one can come to an understanding, and the interaction deteriorates quickly and ends on a sour note. Also, notice how much more complex the nuances of communication are when there is only the virtual encounter, the bare text itself, without any nonverbal component.

Question typed into query box: I wonder, if I have articles, well pages photocopied from a book of short story criticisms, and I have to do a bibliography on it, would I cite the book itself, or individual criticism?

L (Librarian) Hi
L My name is [Lib. First Name], and I'm a reference librarian with the QuestionPoint chat service. Your librarians have asked our librarians to staff this service when they are unavailable. I'm reading your question right now to see how I can
U (User) hey.
L the purpose of a bibliography is so that someone, reading your paper, can go back and find the same sources you
U okay? i know
U thats not what i'm asking
L you would cite the book and probably the page numbers you used
L your source was the book
U okay, so i'm only supposed to cite the book, not individual criticisms
L which citation format are you using
U mla
L MLA citation style uses a simple two-part parenthetical documentation system for citing sources: Citations in the Text of a paper are used to point to an alphabetical Works Cited list that appears at the end of the paper. Together, these references identify and credit the sources used in the paper and allow others to access and retrieve this material.
U know
L in the bibliography you cite the book
U *i know
U that's not what i'm asking
U a simple yes or no

L   in the bibliography you cite the book
U   so just the book, not the individual crticisims from it
L   http://owl.english.purdue.edu/owl/resource/747/01/
L   this is the best web site for MLA citations formattin
U   for the third time
U   that's not what i'm asking
L   for the third time, in the bibliography you cite the book
U   so again . . . JUST the book, nothing else?
L   you might want to ask your teacher how she wants it done
U   oyi, [expletive deleted] it
L   ChatLibrarianEnded.

Even given what should be a simple request, as in the two examples provided above for the bibliography question, as well as the club file instructions, perfect understanding is impossible. John Locke knew that this perfect understanding was impossible too, and spent much time in his *Essay Concerning Human Understanding* explaining why this is so. In the very same paragraph chosen by the OED to represent the transmission view of communication, Locke writes that "when a word stands for a very complex *Idea*, . . . it is not easy for Men to form and retain that *Idea* so exactly, as to make the Name in common use, stand for the same precise *Idea*, without any the least variation" (Locke [1690] 1975, 478).

The whole point of Locke's discussion of communication was to show that it was impossible to express and "send" true ideas from one to another by using words, and how the inherent fallibility of communication was potentially a huge problem for philosophers like himself. After all, suppose a scientist had discovered the truth of what really happened at the beginning of the universe. It would be expressed as a theory, of course, but this one particular theory happened to be correct. Now the scientist must tell the world about her theory but, in order to do this, she must use words. Now we have a problem because the meanings of words are imprecise and ambiguous, and our understanding of a word may not be the same as another's. What do you mean by "universe" anyway? Well, it's a space that is infinitely big. What do you mean by "infinite"? Infinity is something that has no beginning or end. What do you mean by "beginning?" What does the librarian mean in the previous transcript example by "cite?" And so on. Concepts such as "infinity" and "time" are, to use Locke's terms, *complex ideas;* that is, ideas that are not derived directly from experience, but rather created by the mind through combining, distinguishing, compounding, and abstracting other ideas. Because we have no common experience to which we can refer, the interpretation of complex ideas is always relative to the person doing the interpretation, and it is not necessarily the case that people will combine ideas in the same way. Locke pointed out that the names for complex ideas "have seldom, in two different Men, the same precise signification; since one Man's complex *Idea* seldom agrees with another's, and often differs from his own, from that which he had yesterday, or will have tomorrow" (Locke [1690] 1975, 478). So even though we are in possession of an absolutely true idea, the medium of words and language makes it impossible for me to transmit that idea to you *exactly* (to use Locke's word) as it exists in my mind, because I can never be sure that your interpretation of these words is going to be the same as mine. Our transcript example on pages 24–25 is a great illustration of this idea. Why was the library user so frustrated? The interpretation of words was different for each person in that encounter.

We also know Locke's claim to be the case from our own experiences with the dictionary. This book is about "communication"—so far, so good. But what do we mean when we write about "communication"—what do we mean *exactly?* If you look up the word "communication" in the OED (2015), you will find three senses relating to the term: (1) senses relating to affinity or association, (2) senses relating to the imparting or transmission of something, and (3) senses relating to access. Under these three senses, there are a further eighteen subsenses. So it is clear when you read the word "communication" in this text, you are going to have to make a decision about which sense is the most appropriate. In any case, there is no guarantee the sense of communication you interpret is going to be *exactly* (that word again) the same as the one we intended.

For Locke, the answer lies in the nature of words, and of the impossibility of communication as he has described it; that is, as the exact transmission of an idea from a speaker to a hearer. The conclusion to Locke's reflections on language and communication is articulated in his famous lament, that words "interpose themselves so much between our Understandings, and the Truth, which it would contemplate and apprehend, that like the Medium through which visible Objects pass, their Obscurity and Disorder does not seldom cast a mist before our Eyes, and impose upon our Understandings" (Locke [1690] 1975, 488).

It is crucial for us to understand that Locke's transmission account of communication is very much an idealization; it is what Locke *wished* communication could be like, just as we continue to wish communication could be like this today. If only it were possible to understand each other perfectly— what a difference this would make in our lives, from trying to understand our teenage or older adult library users to having the world live in perfect peace and harmony.

Locke is not describing communication in terms of what it is, but rather of what communication would be like if it were possible to transmit ideas perfectly. Locke refers to this ideal form of communication as *philosophical communication.* It refers to such a use of words "as may serve to convey the precise Notions of Things, and to express, in general Propositions, certain and undoubted Truths, which the Mind may rest upon, and be satisfied with, in its search after true knowledge" (Locke [1690] 1975, 476). Even though we can never achieve Locke's philosophical communication in practice (and Locke says as much), it is nevertheless the philosophical use of words that we find in our modern preoccupation with communication as the matching of ideas in a sender and receiver. If communication is to be considered successful, the transfer of ideas needs to be accurate. The idea I hold in my mind must match to some significant degree the idea you hold in your mind. If it does not match, then we have a case of miscommunication. It is this transmission view of communication that lies deep within our culture, and which has come to shape the way we think about communication in our everyday interactions. People believe when they talk to someone, they are sending them their ideas. The same people believe that when they listen to someone speak, they are receiving and understanding the ideas in the mind of the speaker. This is all well and good, but, as Locke has shown us, this is a very poor way to understand what happens in an interpersonal communication encounter.

WHY THE TRANSMISSION VIEW IS A PROBLEM FOR UNDERSTANDING INTERPERSONAL COMMUNICATION: ORAL PRESENTATIONS VERSUS CONVERSATIONS

A central motivation for our belief in the transmission theory of communication is our desire for control. As Carey points out, "communication is a process whereby messages are transmitted and distributed in space for the control of distance and people" (Carey 1992, 15). Ideally, we would all like the ability to *control* communication, *control* communication situations and, perhaps ultimately, to *control* the actions and perceptions of other people, in order to achieve our own objectives and goals. For example, when we speak to others, we may be concerned with creating a "good impression" in the mind of the people to whom we are speaking. We want them to like us or to consider us competent. At work, we may want a supervisor to "understand" how we are feeling right now so we will receive sympathy, support, and so on. For example, in information literacy sessions we may want undergraduates to "understand" that we are approachable when they need research help or have a reference question. The transmission view of communication holds out a tantalizing hope that such control is possible in our communication activities. If we can excite in the mind of a hearer exactly the same idea we have in our mind, in a very important sense we have controlled that person's ideas. We are having them hold ideas that we wish them to hold, and not some other idea. However, John Locke, as far back as 1690, has already demonstrated why this cannot be the case.

There are many areas of communication that work with precisely this philosophy and the goal of manipulating the thoughts and actions of others in ways that are beneficial to the sender. Consider the multibillion-dollar communication industries of advertising, marketing, and public relations. In the area of human communication, the tenets and principles of the transmission theory are most clearly expressed and acted upon in an activity with which we are all very familiar: the giving of an oral presentation.

There are hundreds of textbooks, college courses, and workshops on how to give an effective oral presentation. Many of us may have taken one of these courses, either as part of high school or college education, or as a training requirement in our workplaces. The ability to speak in public is key to our efforts in instruction, program presentation, advocacy, meetings, and giving research papers or workshops at professional conferences. An oral presentation course holds out the promise that if you can control your message, your delivery, and your content, then you can ultimately control, to some extent, the thoughts and actions of your audience members. In an oral presentation, it is the speaker, and the speaker alone, who has the power to shape these outcomes. That is why so much of an oral presentation course is taken up with such things as analyzing the audience, preparing outlines, doing research, and practicing delivery. The audience is there to be informed and persuaded, sitting there to be molded and changed by you. In Locke's idealized philosophical communication, the goal of the presentation is to have the audience take away *exactly* the message you wish them to take away. The more the audience deviates from this ideal, the less effective your speech will be considered and, in the case of students, the worse their grades are going to be.

There are obviously advantages to approaching communication from an oral presentation perspective, which is why so much time and so many resources are dedicated to it. For example, it encourages people to think about their messages ahead of time. It encourages speakers to back up claims with supporting materials, and to have sensitivity to the backgrounds and needs of their audience. Oral presentations draw attention to importance of delivery; that is, how we speak, how we look (dress and appearance), and how we behave (gestures, eye contact, and other nonverbal behaviors). For example, at a springtime state library conference, a prominent library director was overheard saying "the speaker should not wear flip-flops if she wants to be taken seriously." This is an example of how appearance can influence our audience's perception of us. Of greatest importance, however, is the belief that when communication is unsuccessful, you can "fix it" by employing a different and more effective strategy. So your first speech bombed because you spoke too quietly, or you had too much text on your PowerPoint slides, or you did not look directly at the audience, or you failed to establish your credibility as a speaker by wearing flip-flops, and so on. You can fix these things in your next speech, and do much better.

In many ways, this is what people look for when buying books to improve their communication behavior. How can I change what I am doing wrong now, and behave more effectively the second time around? This approach may work very well in an oral presentation situation where the speaker has a great deal of control of what is going on. However, when we apply a transmission/oral presentation approach to interpersonal communication, we will find that things do not work out so well. The mistake we make in thinking about communication is that we try and impose a transmission/oral presentation mindset onto conversational situations. The simple fact is that a conversation is very different from an oral presentation. You cannot control the content of a conversation in the same way you can control the content of an oral presentation.

In short, we need to give up our belief in a transmission view of communication if we wish to understand interpersonal communication in useful ways. Perhaps James Carey made the point most forcefully when he wrote:

> The transmission view of communication has dominated American thought since the 1920s. When I first came into this field I felt that this view of communication, expressed in behavioral and functional terms, was exhausted. It has become academic: a repetition of past achievement, a demonstration of the indubitable. Although it led to solid achievement, it could no longer go forward without disastrous intellectual and social consequences. (Carey 1992, 23)

One goal of this book is to raise skepticism or perhaps even overturn the transmission view of communication, because it is, in many ways, an impediment to understanding human communication. Clearly, we need a different way to articulate and understand interpersonal communication if we are to make meaningful changes in how we communicate. Thankfully, such a view is available, as we shall see in the following section.

LOCKE'S CIVIL COMMUNICATION AND GADAMER'S GENUINE CONVERSATION

If conversation is different from an oral presentation, how are we to conceive of conversations that would be of value to information professionals? There is such a viewpoint, which can be found in the dictionary, right next door to the transmission view of communication as exemplified by John Locke's quotation. If you examine the definitions of "communication" found in the OED (2015), it is surprising to learn that the transmission view of communication is quite low in a long list of different meanings. You will also find that the etymology of the term "communication" has less to do with transmission and much more to do with interpersonal communication and practical wisdom. For example, in the late thirteenth century, the term "communication" referred to "interpersonal contact," "social interaction," and "the fact of having something in common with another person." In the early fourteenth century, "communication" referred to "participation in the Eucharist" and "the action of taking communion." In the sixteenth century, "communication" appears in texts where it used to refer to "the action of sharing in something" and "mutual participation." James Carey refers to this use of the term "communication" as a kind of social action as the *ritual view of communication.* In this view, "communication" is firmly linked to terms such as "sharing," "participation," and "association" rather than "transmission." It draws a direct line from its roots of "commonness," "communion," and "community" in ways that the OED now lists as archaic. As Carey describes: "A ritual view of communication is directed not toward the extension of messages in space but toward the maintenance of society in time; not the act of imparting information but the representation of shared beliefs" (Carey 1992, 18). Emanating from these early religious frames, the archetypal case of "communication" is not the sender transmitting a message to the receiver (such as giving an oral presentation), but the sacred ceremony that draws people together in fellowship and commonality, such as Holy Communion in a church service. In the ritual view, importance is placed upon the role of community prayer, singing, and ceremony, that is, upon the activities that people perform *together,* and not upon the individual priest who gives a sermon to a congregation.

Although John Locke was also very aware of the ritual functions of words and social interaction, in his account of communication he referred to the everyday action of communication as *civil communication.* He defines *civil communication* as "such a communication of Thoughts and Ideas by Words, as may serve for the upholding common Conversation and Commerce, about the ordinary Affairs and Conveniences of civil life, in the Societies of Men, one amongst another" (Locke [1690] 1975, 476). Here the point of communication is not to transmit an idea from a sender to a receiver, but rather the "upholding of conversation." In other words, communication in its civil sense allows people to engage in conversations and recognizes that they are important in their own right, and not just as means of transmitting ideas from one point to another.

For example, think about the last time you phoned a friendly colleague at work. There you are, talking away, and the next thing you know twenty or so minutes have gone by and you are now late for a meeting or a shift on the service desk. Where did that time go? It seemed to pass by so quickly. So what happened in the time that went by so quickly? Sometimes it is hard to tell. Perhaps, you began by phoning your colleague to discuss an upcoming library program or to ask a quick question. You began on point, but before you know it, you were talking about all kinds of other, unrelated topics: a different project or upcoming deadline, what you are going to do this weekend, a novel you are reading, and so on. Sometimes you find yourself disclosing information or personal feelings that you never really intended to reveal. As you find yourself moving from one topic to the next, you get the sense that this conversation has developed its own flow and you have been caught up in its meandering currents. It takes you to places that you would never have imagined or predicted when the conversation started. Unlike an oral presentation (where you have more control over what is said and when), in a conversation (like the one described above) it almost seems as if the conversation is controlling you.

In a conversation like this, you are going to start inventing actions together that neither of you planned in advance. It will start to take on a life of its own in which both of you seem to be responding to something that is emerging in front of you. It is unclear who is leading or following, or how you ever got to what you were talking about. What you are experiencing is something like the quality of good conversational jazz. A jazz session will begin with a structured musical sequence in which the musicians can get comfortable with each other, but all of a sudden the musicians get "in the groove," and each begins to improvise. Music is being played that could not have been played before, because it is not in the heads of any of the individual musicians. It is as if the music is demanding more music to respond to it. The music being created in the moment has this quality of going somewhere, but we do not know beforehand where it is supposed to go. It is the experience of a conversation like this that hermeneutic philosopher Hans-Georg Gadamer has referred to as a "genuine conversation." Gadamer's description of the genuine conversation is worth quoting in full:

We say that we "conduct" a conversation, but the more genuine a conversation is, the less its conduct lies within the will of either partner. Thus a genuine conversation is never the one that we wanted to conduct. Rather, it is generally more correct to say that we fall into conversation, or even that we become involved in it. The way one word follows another, with the conversation taking its own twists and reaching its own conclusion, may well be conducted in some way, but the partners conversing are far less the leaders of it than the led. No one knows in advance what will "come out" of a conversation. Understanding or its failure is like an event that happens to us. (Gadamer 1989, 383)

It is not intellectually satisfying to describe and explain the experience of a genuine conversation in terms of an oral presentation where one person is attempting to control the responses of another person. The experience of the genuine conversation is much more than this. Gadamer suggests that the conversation is more of a game, like tennis or chess, where the players have become totally absorbed in its continual back-and-forth movement. The game is not being directed by what is going on inside the players' minds. As Gadamer (1976a, 66) points out, we must "free ourselves from the customary mode of thinking that considers the nature of the game from the point of view of the consciousness of the player." The real subject of playing is the game itself. All playing is, in fact, a kind of "being played," where the participants are often surprised by what they find themselves to be doing or saying at any particular point. Gadamer (1976b, 57) proposes that "it cannot be denied that in an actual dialogue of this kind something of the character of accident, favor, and surprise—and, in the end, of buoyancy, indeed, of elevation—that belongs to the nature of the game that is present."

To attempt to control a genuine conversation would be like trying to swim against a very strong current. You may want the conversation to go in a particular direction, but the conversation itself constantly pushes you back. The same is the case intellectually; the genuine conversation resists our attempts to impose a transmission theory to describe and explain it.

Think through the consequences of what would happen if you did try to control the flow of a conversation. What would happen in a conversation where one person deliberately dictates what is said, how it is said, when it is said? Our gut reaction is that such a situation would immediately lead to very negative responses and perceptions from your conversational partner. We tend to keep away from people who try to dominate and control our conversations, those who do not allow us to respond or put limits on how we should or should not respond. And yet this is exactly the philosophy of communication we buy into when we purchase "how to communicate" books based on a transmission/oral presentation view of communication. We have this bizarre belief that we can solve our communication problems by "doing communication right," as if such a thing actually existed in a conversational realm. Such a philosophy may work very well for an oral presentation. However, in that situation, the people to whom you are speaking are sitting quietly and attentively, you have the floor and get to control the content and the delivery—all with the willing consent of your audience members. But in a conversation, these people are going to talk back to you, and you will need to continually devise new strategies, from moment to moment, depending on what the other person is doing or saying.

In a genuine conversation, no matter how clearly you speak, no matter how expansively you gesture, no matter how much eye contact you give the other person, you cannot directly control how the other is going to interpret and respond to those behaviors. For example, what you consider to be a friendly smile intended to put your conversational partner at ease could easily be interpreted as patronizing, insincere, or just downright creepy. Indeed, your smiling behavior may do more harm than good and elicit a response completely opposite to the one you intended. In live chat reference, for example, typing a simple closing statement such as "good luck" can be misinterpreted as a "good-bye and don't come back" dismissal, rather than as an encouragement. The key to a practical approach to thinking about interpersonal communication is to realize that we must manage our expectations about how much we will be able to control communication in a conversation. We are not giving a speech here. We will not be in a position of total control. We must be prepared to be comfortable in knowing that not every communication situation will go perfectly, every time, and that there are things that will always be beyond our control.

AN EXAMPLE

Let us give a longer library-related example that ties up the main points of this chapter: (a) that the transmission theory is an inadequate means of describing and explaining interpersonal communication, and (b) that we need a theory of interpersonal communication that will acknowledge and account for the game-like, jazz-performance-like, nature of genuine conversation.

Consider the following situation: this is your first month as director of a medium-sized urban public library. You are just getting to know your staff and are spending time on the library floor, observing the type and level of service at the circulation desk. You notice that Jen, a staff member who has worked at the library for six years, is talking on the phone, the receiver tucked under her neck, while she simultaneously checks out books to a line of people. Jen does not greet or make eye contact with the users. She just robotically scans the books and hands them back without a smile. Sometime later, you see Jen and say, "I notice that you are on the phone while serving people at the circulation desk." Jen replies brightly, "Yes, I do that all the time. I'm multitasking. I managed to clear up a scheduling conflict today."

In a view of communication based on the transmission of messages, we might say the manager has an idea (to tell Jen to be more attentive to the library users), the manager puts this idea into words ("Jen, you must be more attentive to the library users"), and then the manager transmits this message to Jen through speech. In an ideal world (where Locke's philosophical communication actually existed), Jen would receive the message, understand the idea sent by the manager, and immediately change her behavior accordingly. But we can see right away how unsophisticated this account is. We know from our experience that people simply do not respond to single messages in predictable ways; they participate and act in sequences of messages we know as conversations. The manager's message would be part of a conversation, or at least it would initiate a conversation in which Jen would be expected to respond in some way. The manager's idea is not simply transmitted or injected into Jen's head. The meanings and implications of the message have to be negotiated in the form of a conversation. The manager has to take into account how Jen might react to the message, not simply in terms of the information or the idea in the manager's mind, but also in terms of how Jen might interpret what the message says about her, as a person. Jen may interpret the message to mean that she is personally incompetent. She may think that, by deliberately picking out this one incident, the manager does not appreciate the good work Jen does the rest of the time. It may alter Jen's perception of her own creativity or initiative when she chooses to multitask at the service desk in order to accomplish different tasks simultaneously. The message may cause Jen to form a negative first impression of the manager, which could lead to unproductive and dysfunctional interactions in the future. There is so much more to be read into the manager's message, "Jen, you must be more attentive to the patrons," than a simple, "this is an idea in my head that I want you to adopt." A transmission view of communication can tell you how the message moved from point A (the manager) to point B (Jen), but it cannot explain the complexities and consequences of this one message on a whole host of other things (feelings, impressions, future interactions, etc.).

This simple exchange between Jen and the library manager does much to reveal the shortcomings of a transmission approach to interpersonal communication. The transmission view attempts to fix and separate the roles of the sender and the receiver. We want to see the manager as the sender, and we want to understand the communication process as one in which she conveys her message successfully to Jen. But interpersonal communication between two people always involves simultaneous sending and receiving, as well as message interpretation. Even as the manager is sending her message to Jen, Jen is at the same time sending messages back to the manager, which the manager is obliged to respond to in some way. By responding to Jen, it is clear the manager is not, and cannot be, in total control of what happens in the conversation, not even her own behaviors, because she must respond to what Jen is doing and saying, and not simply to the ideas, desires, and objectives in her own head.

A transmission view of communication constructs the sender of the message as the active decision maker who determines the meaning of the message, and the receiver as the passive target of the message. However, Jen is not passive here. She has her own thoughts and desires, and her own messages she wishes to communicate to the manager. Her statement, "Yes, I do that all the time. I'm multitasking. I managed to clear up a scheduling conflict today," is possibly intended to communicate to the manager that Jen is doing a good job and is seeking her manager's praise. There is no provision in a transmission view of communication to give feedback like this or to take into account the relationship of the participants in a conversation. All we know about Jen and the manager is what we have learned in this one brief interaction. But what is their working relationship like? Have they had positive interactions in the past, or negative ones? Do they have positive or negative perceptions of each other? The history of Jen and the manager's relationship will have a significant bearing on how the messages in this brief interaction will be understood and acted upon, but a transmission view fails to consider these aspects. A transmission view of communication is unable to incorporate any sense of what the people in this conversation, or any conversation, are actually talking *about*. All it can do is describe and explain the means by which the people are sending information to one another. It does not take into account that people change over time, or that relationships and contexts change, or how a message may mean something in one context and something totally different in another. The transmission view does not address how the medium of communication impacts the potential meaning of a message. What would the message mean to Jen if the manager had communicated her concerns by e-mail or a formal memo, or indirectly through a conversation with the head of circulation that is then relayed to Jen, or in a meeting in front of other circulation staff members?

In short, even though a transmission view dominates our common-sense understandings, as a means of understanding our interpersonal communication encounters it falls significantly short. It fails to account for times when the message sent does not equal the message that is received. Indeed, if we attempted to follow transmission-view principles in our own interpersonal communication encounters, they would become dysfunctional quite quickly. Again, the key drawback centers in our belief that Locke's idealization of communication, that is, Locke's Holy Grail of true philosophical communication, the belief that other people can understand our ideas *exactly* as we intended them, is, in fact, something that can be achieved in reality.

So when inevitably others do not understand our ideas exactly as we want them to, we are tempted to seek a cause. Let us assume that following the multitasking encounter at the reference desk, the manager subsequently gives Jen a below-average performance review. Jen might say to her manager, "I thought I was doing a good job. It is your fault I got a poor evaluation because you did not express your expectations clearly." The supervisor might say, "It is your fault your evaluation is poor, because you did not listen to me when I asked you to be more attentive to library users at the circulation desk, and you failed to seek clarification of what these expectations actually meant." In a scenario such as this, our concept of communication has become overly linear and causal. We believe communication moves from A (the manager) to B (the employee) and that any problems with the successful transmission of these ideas lies either with the source (you were not clear) or the destination (you were not listening). As we can see, both of the people involved can claim the failure to communicate is the fault of the other. This does not necessarily solve any communication problems or issues that might exist between Jen and her manager. The most it can do is give both participants a strategy to maintain face in an encounter where both participants have the potential to create bad impressions that may have long-lasting effects on their relationship.

This chapter has put forward the flaws in taking a transmission view of communication in interpersonal situations, and has provided some examples to illustrate these shortcomings. The next chapters begin to unfold an alternative view that may forever change our perception of interpersonal communication in professional (and personal) situations.

REFERENCES

Aristotle. 2004. *The Nicomachean Ethics.* Translated by James Alexander Kerr Thomson. New York: Penguin Books.

Bronowski, Jacob. 1973. *The Ascent of Man.* New York: Little, Brown and Company.

Carey, James. 1992. *Communication as Culture.* New York: Routledge.

Gadamer, Hans-Georg. 1976a. "Man and Language." Translated by David E. Linge. In *Philosophical Hermeneutics,* edited by David E. Linge, 59–68. Berkeley, CA: University of California Press.

Gadamer, Hans-Georg. 1976b. *"On the Problem of Self-Understanding."* Translated by David E. Linge. In *Philosophical Hermeneutics,* edited by David E. Linge, 44–58. Berkeley, CA: University of California Press.

———. 1989. *Truth and Method,* 2nd revised edition. Joel Weinsheimer and Donald Marshall, New York: Continuum.

Goffman, Erving. 1967. *Interaction Ritual: Essays on Face-to-Face Behavior.* Garden City, New York: Doubleday.

Lakoff, George, and Mark Johnson. 1980. *Metaphors We Live By.* Chicago: University of Chicago Press.

Locke, John. [1690] 1975. *An Essay Concerning Human Understanding,* edited by Peter H. Nidditch. Oxford, UK: Clarendon Press.

Oxford English Dictionary. 2015. "Communication, N." *OED Online.* October 2015. Oxford University Press. Available: www.oed.com.

Pearce, Barnett. 1994. *Interpersonal Communication: Making Social Worlds.* New York: Harper Collins.

Radford, Marie L. 1993. "Relational Aspects of Reference Interactions: A Qualitative Investigation of the Perceptions of Users and Librarians in the Academic Library." PhD diss., Rutgers, The State University of New Jersey.

———. 1999. *The Reference Encounter: Interpersonal Communication in the Academic Library.* Chicago: Association of College and Research Libraries.

Radford, Marie L., and Lynn S. Connaway. 2005–2008. *Seeking Synchronicity: Evaluating Virtual Reference Services from User, Non-User, and Librarian Perspectives.* Dublin, OH: OCLC Research, 2008. www.oclc.org/research/themes/user-studies/synchronicity.html.

Radford, Marie L., Lynn S. Connaway, and Chirag Shah. 2011–2014. *Cyber Synergy: Seeking Sustainability through Collaboration between Virtual Reference and Social Q&A Sites.* OCLC Research, 2014. www.oclc.org/research/activities/synergy/default.htm.

Radford, M. L., Radford, G. P., Connaway, L. S., and DeAngelis, J. A. October, 2011. "On Virtual Face-Work: An Ethnography of Communication Approach to a Live Chat Reference Interaction." *The Library Quarterly* 81 (4), 431–53.

Reddy, Michael J. 1979. "The Conduit Metaphor: A Case of Frame Conflict in Our Language about Language." In *Metaphor and Thought,* edited by Andrew Ortony. Cambridge, UK: Cambridge University Press.

Shannon, Claude E. 1949. "The Mathematical Theory of Communication." In *The Mathematical Theory of Communication,* by Claude E. Shannon and Warren Weaver, 31–125. Urbana, IL: University of Illinois Press.

NOTE

1. Radford and Connaway (2005–2008) and Radford, Connaway, and Shah (2011–2014) collected two random samples of live-chat transcripts from a large pool of sessions from OCLC's QuestionPoint service (www.questionpoint.org), an international provider of chat software for library VR services (VRS). Prior to analysis, all information that could identify librarians and library users was removed. Transcript analysis used a method developed by Radford and Connaway (2005–2008) and Radford, Radford, Connaway, and DeAngelis (2011) that identified a number of face-work categories following Goffman (1967). Transcripts are presented verbatim.

A Relational View of Interpersonal Communication

Reclaiming Ruesch and Bateson's
Communication: The Social Matrix of Psychiatry

*When A communicates with B, the mere act of communicating can carry the implicit
statement "we are communicating." In fact, this may be the most important message
that is sent and received.*

—RUESCH AND BATESON ([1951] 1968, 213)

C hapter 2 described the transmission theory of communication in
some depth, and explored how it has come to dominate our common-sense understanding of interpersonal communication. We also
examined the shortcomings of such a view and the reasons we need
to rethink our approach to interpersonal communication if we are to improve
relationships in the library workplace. From as long ago as Aristotle some
300 years BC and John Locke in 1690, it has been recognized that communication can be categorized and understood in terms of two fundamentally
different conceptual approaches. Aristotle articulated the distinction in terms
of the scientific versus the practical, whereas Locke distinguished between the
philosophical and the civil. Carey (1992) adds to this his distinction between
transmission and ritual communication. However, in our scholarship and in
our culture, it is the scientific, philosophical, and transmission views that have
informed our dominant understandings of interpersonal communication. It is
Locke's *philosophical* characterization of communication that appears in the
Oxford English Dictionary (OED) (2015) definitions, and not his description of
civil communication. It is the *ritual* senses of communication that are listed

as "archaic" in the OED, and not the *transmission* senses. However, we assert that a transmission view of interpersonal communication is not a particularly useful way to understand or improve our interpersonal communication encounters. Rather, we need to reclaim a practical, civil, and ritual path and elevate Locke's concept of civil communication into the forethought of our thinking about interpersonal communication. We see this shift happening in communication scholarship (see Pearce 1994), but very little of this perspective has spilled over into the realm of understanding the everyday interactions of real people, in real relationships, with real goals, and occurring in real situations. We intend to offer a much-needed corrective.

CONVERSATION AND MUTUAL UNDERSTANDING

The first thing we have to do is consider interpersonal communication through the frame of a metaphor different from that of communication as transmission or as a conduit. As we have seen, the metaphors underlying the dominant transmission view are that of *movement* (of messages from one point to another) and *control* (of the effect of those messages on others). What would happen if we replaced these guiding metaphors with others that better reflect a more practical approach (in Aristotle's sense) and recognize the importance of conversation for its own sake; that is, as something other than trying to impose one's will or ideas on another person?

Jurgen Habermas's account of communication is relevant here. His theory of communicative action looks at "how language has the ability to coordinate action in a consensual or cooperative way as opposed to a forced or manipulated one" (Warnke 1995, 120). Habermas differentiates between two motives that underlie interpersonal communication. The first he calls the "orientation towards success," which reflects much of our discussion of the transmission theory approach to interpersonal communication. Habermas writes:

> If the actors are interested solely in the *success,* i.e., the *consequences* or *outcomes* of their actions, they will try to reach their objectives by influencing their opponent's definition of the situation, and thus his decisions or motives, through external means by using weapons or goods, threats or enticements. Such actors treat each other *strategically.* (Habermas 1990, 133)

Of interest to us is Habermas's contrast to strategic action, which he calls "communicative action." Habermas writes:

By contrast, I speak of *communicative* action when actors are prepared to harmonize their plans of action through internal means, committing themselves to pursuing their goals only on the condition of an agreement—one that already exists or one to be negotiated—about definitions of the situation and prospective outcomes. (Habermas 1990, 134)

Our approach will be to recognize the conversation as important, and not just the individual aims of the conversant. The goal of a conversation is not to control or influence the behaviors of the other person, but to create the conditions where both people can achieve "mutual understanding." This mutual understanding includes shared definitions of the situation (what is going on) on which both people can agree and then can engage in making changes based on that understanding.

The principle of mutual understanding, whereby understanding is created together, rather than being created by one person and transmitted to another, is captured in the metaphor of Escher's famous *Drawing Hands* (see figure 3.1). In this sketch, the action of the first hand makes possible the existence and

FIGURE 3.1

M. C. Escher's *Drawing Hands*

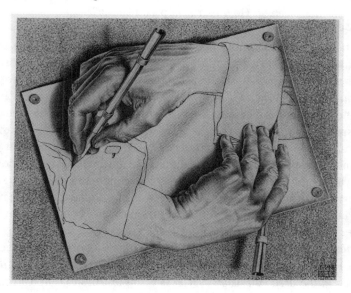

action of the second hand. However, it is the action of the second hand that makes possible the existence and action of the first hand.

The same principle informs a view of interpersonal communication seen from the perspective of a conversation rather than message transmission. In a conversation, the behavior of B is a function of (a response to) the behavior of A. However, the behavior of A is also a function of (and response to) the behavior of B. In other words, the sender A is not, and, indeed, cannot be, the sole determinant of what she does and says, because what she does and says is always contingent upon the actions of the other person.

How might this metaphor help in understanding the dynamics of a library encounter? Consider this example that takes place at the reserve desk in an academic library. In this example, a graduate student (Jo) is doing research on a historical approach to gender issues in American History textbooks. She approaches the reserve desk, and asks for a particular text that has been put on reserve for undergraduate students. The access services librarian (Pam) is on her way to a meeting when the student assistant stops her and asks her to speak to Jo, who wants to borrow the text on reserve.

Scenario 1

Pam: *Speaks calmly, but not in the best of moods, thinking that now she will surely be late for her meeting.* How can I help you today?

Jo: I need to borrow this book, but the student said this is on reserve and I can't take it home. I simply must be able to take it home. I expect that it will take me several weeks to do a close content analysis of these images and the text that goes with them for my thesis.

Pam: *Firm tone.* I'm sorry, but this book is on reserve. You are welcome to use it in the library, but it cannot be borrowed for any length of time until the semester is over. You are not the only person who needs to use this book.

Jo: *Becoming upset and raising her voice.* That's just great, this is not going to help me, I have kids at home and am unable to stay for long periods of time in the library. I'm on a tight timetable to complete my thesis this semester.

Pam: *Unsympathetic, firm.* Sorry, but that is our policy. Perhaps the reference librarian can help you find another edition of this book or a similar book to use?

Jo: *Indignant.* I need *this* one, as I said I'm taking a historical approach. (*Frustrated.*) This is so typical. (*Turns around and raises her voice, so that other students in the area can hear her.*) Every single time I come to this library I am always given the runaround. (*Walks away upset.*)

We could view this example in two ways:

1. From the perspective of communication as strategic action, we can say that it is the responsibility of the access services librarian, Pam, to *control* Jo's attitudes and behaviors by sending her a message and have her *comply* with the library policy of not circulating books that are on reserve. The librarian might do this by quoting the rule book ("this is our policy"); by shaming Jo (by saying "you are not the only person who needs this book," which implies that Jo would be selfish to take the book away from other students who also need it), or simply by pulling rank ("I am the librarian, you must comply because these are the rules").

2. From the perspective of interpersonal communication in terms of communicative action, we can say that it is the responsibility of the librarian to engage Jo in a conversation with the goal of reaching a mutual *understanding* of the situation and of why her behavior might be considered inappropriate or selfish. Ideally, this conversation will help Jo *to understand* how her behavior affects others.

Upon reflection, the conversation took a negative turn quickly, and Jo has reacted to the denial of her request and Pam's sour tone that indicates a lack of empathy for Jo's situation (which implies that Jo is selfish, thus shaming her). Feeling shamed and frustrated, Jo then becomes upset and acts out by loudly denouncing the library to all within earshot. Rather than simply being the transmission of a relatively simple and clearly stated message ("this book is on reserve, it cannot be borrowed") from sender to receiver, this encounter has taken on a complexity that goes beyond the mere delivery of this information.

Now, let's consider a second version of this scenario.

Scenario 2

Pam: *Speaks calmly, but not in the best of moods, thinking that now she will surely be late for her meeting.* How can I help you today?

Jo: I need to borrow this book, but the student said this is on reserve and I can't take it home. I simply must be able to take it home. I expect that it will take me several weeks to do a close content analysis of these images and the text that goes with them for my thesis.

Pam: *Sympathetic tone.* I'm sorry, but this book is on reserve. You are welcome to use it in the library, but it simply cannot be borrowed for any length of time until the semester is over.

Jo: *Pleading tone.* That is not going to help me. I have kids at home and am unable to stay for long periods of time in the library. I'm on a tight time-table to complete my thesis this semester.

Pam: *Conciliatory.* Ok, let's think about this. There is an alternative if you don't need the book today.

Jo: *Brightening.* This is a semester-long project, I don't need this book imme-diately, but I do need to borrow it for about two weeks for my analysis.

Pam: *Upbeat.* Ok in that case, we can interlibrary loan this book. I am sure we can find another library that can send it within a week to ten days.

Jo: *Grateful and smiling.* Really? Thanks so much. That would be perfect.

Looked at this way, the conversation between Pam and Jo begins to appear less like a series of commands and more similar to the type of conversation that might take place between a therapist and a patient, where the goal of the conversation is not control, but rather achieving mutual understanding of a problematic situation and working out a viable and collaborative resolution (see also Fine 1995). In this case, one way to understand this conversation would be to take the stance that Pam needs to "diagnose" the situation and come up with a negotiated solution that will satisfy Jo, which at the same time would also be in compliance with library policies regarding reserve books. In the second scenario, Pam does this successfully by including Jo in the identi-fication of an alternative that enables everyone to maintain self-esteem, build good relationships, and achieve a positive outcome. Can our understanding of library conversations be further enlightened by theoretical approaches that are grounded in psychiatry, and that later develop into the relational view of interpersonal communication? We believe that they can.

This linking of interpersonal communication with psychiatric conversations was developed most forcefully by Jurgen Ruesch and Gregory Bateson (1968) in *Communication: The Social Matrix of Psychiatry,* first published in 1951. A book published in 1951 may seem an odd choice to appear in a modern treatment of interpersonal communication. However, the timing of the book and its impact on our understanding of interpersonal communication is itself instructive because, like this work, it stood in contrast to the prevailing trans-mission view of communication. Ruesch and Bateson's book appeared at a pivotal time in the history of communication theory and research. Shannon and Weaver's *The Mathematical Theory of Communication,* published in 1949, was instrumental in constructing the scientific (in Aristotle's sense) founda-tions of a sender-message-receiver (transmission) view of communication that remains dominant in communication scholarship to this day. Ruesch and Bateson's account of communication offered a stark contrast to this view, and continues to go against the grain of our thinking about communication even now. Who today would speak about interpersonal communication in the professional setting in terms of therapy? We are more accustomed to talking about interpersonal communication as a means of transmitting or exchanging ideas, making our messages more effective, or making our behaviors motivating, rather than in terms of pathologies and therapy. This approach makes it sound as if the people involved in the communication were patients, and that they were deficient in some way. However, we assert that it is not the *people* involved in interpersonal encounters who are deficient; it is *the communication itself* that requires diagnosis. Ruesch and Bateson's crucial insight was that the processes of interpersonal communication can be analyzed quite apart from the psychologies of the people involved. This is a crucial claim that we will explore and explain in the following sections.

FROM TRANSMISSION TO THERAPY: TWO WAYS OF THINKING ABOUT COMMUNICATION

The impetus for Ruesch and Bateson's ([1951] 1968) work was the psychiatric treatment of soldiers returning to the United States from the battlefields of World War II. These scholars saw in communication a concept that could help them in their endeavors. In the preface to the 1968 edition of their book, Ruesch and Bateson on explicitly referred to the work of Claude Shannon as a major stimulus for their approach to interpersonal communication when they wrote that the mathematical theory of communication is perhaps the "most exciting scientific and intellectual innovation in the twentieth century" (Ruesch and Bateson 1968, v). However, Ruesch and Bateson saw in the concept of communication something quite different from that articulated by Shannon and Weaver. This difference is central to the claims about interpersonal communication made here. Ruesch and Bateson made the bold statement that "at the time this book was written, it became abundantly clear that the age of the individual had passed, and that psychological man was dead and social man had taken his place" (Ruesch and Bateson 1968, vi). Ruesch and Bateson's claims about the end of the age of the individual and the death of psychological man sound as strange today as they probably did in 1968. These insights contradict our dominant view of communication as "a sender transmitting a message to a receiver." We are simply accustomed to believing that the essence of communication is that an individual has an idea, and she transmits it, by speech, writing, or some other medium, to another individual, who then shares that idea.

Ruesch and Bateson's approach is driven by the notion of *feedback* rather than *transmission.* This distinction is important in psychiatry because of the presence of the psychiatrist, who seeks to elicit *feedback* from the patient, rather than simply generating *responses.* The feedback from the patient allows the therapist to pose new questions, which in turn generate more feedback. The patient's feedback is shaped by the psychiatrist's questions, but, in turn, the psychiatrist's questions are shaped by the patient's feedback. If we consider the example above in scenario 2, feedback was critical to discovering the solution that was successful for both Jo and Pam. The information provided by Jo that, although she needed to take home that particular book, she did *not* need it immediately, opened up the possibility of an interlibrary loan that was missing from scenario 1. This option could not be considered without Jo's response in reply to Pam's invitation to collaborate: "Ok, let's think about this. There is an alternative if you don't need the book today." The idea of feedback allows Jo to be a player in co-constructing a creative and collaborative resolution. In fact, many times there is a pivotal moment in our encounters with library users and colleagues that hinges on the possibilities that are opened by this collaborative moment. If participants are aware of this option, often a successful solution can be found, rather than continual reenactment of knee-jerk reactions that involve evoking policy and procedures that focus on control (of materials, borrowing practices, bureaucratic rules, etc.) (see Radford and Radford 2005). The mindset that control of conversations and behaviors within the library is possible and desirable has pervaded our thinking, and our focus on information delivery as primary to library encounters (see Radford 1999).

It is argued here that this is a consequence of the transmission view that places emphasis on the prediction and control of the responses of a receiver. However, we want to consider a view that sees conversation as a means of self-reflection, insight, and behavioral change, which can be compared to that of the psychiatrist and patient. The psychiatrist does not *cause* this change—rather she attempts to create *the conditions* in which a patient may bring change about for herself, or not. In order to facilitate such change in the patient, Ruesch and Bateson's crucial move, and the move we wish to make in this book, is to recognize *the interaction between the therapist and patient* as the unit of analysis, rather than the psychologies of the individuals involved. We propose that successful or effective interpersonal communication is not about changing the psychology of another person. It is not about using strategies to get what you want. It is not about controlling the responses of another person in ways that benefit the sender. It *is* about creating the communicative conditions in which change becomes possible. This is the leap we are asking you, the reader, to make with us, just as Ruesch and Bateson did in 1951.

CONTENT AND RELATIONAL ASPECTS OF COMMUNICATION

Ruesch and Bateson proposed a cybernetic approach to conversation; that is, one that integrates feedback. This approach embraces the idea that interpersonal communication is much more than simply transmitting messages back and forth. Communication can also be described and understood as a sequence of behaviors that is *interdependent;* that is, the behaviors and utterances of each person are contingent upon the other and become linked in systematic ways. This interdeterminacy, or linking, therefore implies a commitment from the participants to take into account the actions of the other, while creating actions of their own, and which, in Watzlawick, Beavin Bavelas, and Jackson's terms, "defines a relationship" (Watzlawick, Beavin Bavelas, and Jackson 1967, 51). Interpersonal communication, then, not only conveys information, *it also imposes behavior.*

Ruesch and Bateson proposed that each message in a conversation has two sorts of meaning: "On the one hand, the message is a statement or report about events at a previous moment, and on the other hand it is a command—a cause or stimulus for events at a later moment" (Ruesch and Bateson [1951] 1968, 179). They offer the famous example of three neurons: A, B, and C. The firing of neuron A leads to the firing of neuron B. In turn, the firing of neuron B leads to the firing of neuron C.

Firing of neuron A → (causes) → firing of neuron B →
(causes) → firing of neuron C

Consider the meanings of the message transmitted from neuron B to neuron C. The first meaning is a *report* to C that neuron A has fired (because B cannot fire until A has fired). The second meaning is a command that neuron C should now fire. The message tells C that something has happened in the past, and that it should now do something in the future. Ruesch and Bateson ([1951] 1968, 180) claim that "the same is true of all verbal communication and indeed of all communication whatsoever." The leap from an example about hypothetical neurons to "all verbal communication" may seem like a large one, but let us consider what Ruesch and Bateson are proposing and how it will apply to interpersonal communication in professional settings.

Most people will be familiar with the report function. In a conversation, each message is a report of something that has occurred in the past and caused this message to be sent. We often say that the message is a report on the thoughts or perceptions of the sender. Participants in a conversation might report that "the weather is bad," or "the New York Jets actually play in New Jersey," or "our live chat virtual reference consortium requires that we contribute eight hours of staff service per week." These messages "report" the state of the weather, or the geographical location of the old Giants Stadium (now MetLife Stadium), or the staffing requirements of our consortium. A transmission (sender-receiver) view of communication favors the report function in its account of interpersonal interactions. It sees communication as the transmission of content from one person to another. The purpose of the interaction is to ensure that this movement of information takes place successfully, and has the desired effect. Self-help approaches to interpersonal communication might consider the problems that could hinder the report in its movement from sender to receiver, such as distractions in the environment, lack of attention on the part of the listener, or inappropriate use of language on the part of the sender.

What distinguishes Ruesch and Bateson's view of communication is that each message in an interaction is also a *command* that indicates to the other person what kind of response it is appropriate to give. So if I say "the weather is bad," an appropriate response from you might be, "yes, we may have to cancel our annual library picnic later." An inappropriate response would be for you to look away and stay silent. This is why my message is described as a "command"—my utterance compels you to behave in return, just as the firing of neuron B compels neuron C to fire. So my statement both tells you something (content or information) and also gives direction as to what you should do and say in response.

Now, obviously, my saying "the weather is bad" does not allow me to command and control your response in any direct way. There are any number of things you may say in response, such as, "Oh yes, how awful," or "We'd better inform the staff about the picnic's cancellation," or "We need to see if we can move indoors." However, my message has not been conveyed in a conversational vacuum. There is a reason I should mention the state of the weather at that given point in time. Given our relationship and past history, it is probable that my statement about the weather is also a statement about the library picnic that may or may not be occurring later in the day. So my statement about the weather is not only a report on the conditions outside, it is also a report on a whole history of past conversations and activities, such as our planning for the picnic. In other words, it is a report on the fact we have a relationship that has developed over time and over many previous conversations. We are in this conversation because we stand in a particular relationship with each other. My message both reports that and creates it. The response you give will be a report on my message (i.e., the fact you said "yes, we may have to cancel our picnic later," is a report to me that you have received my message "the weather is bad.") At the same time, your response has continued the conversation, and your response has reinforced the status of our relationship. As Ruesch and Bateson famously observed: "When A communicates with B, the mere act of communicating can carry the implicit statement 'we are communicating.' In fact, this may be the most important message that is sent and received" ([1951] 1968, 213). Added to this message is the important implication that we are communicating because we stand in a particular relationship with one another.

This command aspect of conversation is of equal, if not greater, importance than the report aspect (see Radford 1999, 1993 for research in academic libraries that explores and illustrates this idea). Our conversations speak more about "us" (e.g., our experiences, our beliefs, our personalities) than they do about "our thoughts." Rusech and Bateson write that "the conversations of our leisure hours exist because people need to know they are in touch with others" ([1951] 1968, 213). My statement about the weather being bad may indeed be a report on my thoughts at this particular moment in time, but it is also a message that says "I share your concern about the picnic," or that "we have looked forward to the library picnic for so long, it's a shame it may get cancelled," and ultimately that "we plan and do things together." In other words, the act of communication is as important as the content of communication. It is a statement about our relationship.

Ruesch and Bateson refer to this aspect of interpersonal communication as "metacommunication" which is defined as "communication about communication" ([1951] 1968, 209). In the conversation example above, my statement about the weather is not only about the weather, it is also about our status as a dyad. For example, I could have modified my statement to say, "the weather is bad, Dean Jones." The addition of the formal title "Dean" does not add to the content of the message (it is still a report on the state of the weather), but it does say something about our relationship and how we stand with respect to each other. As Ruesch and Bateson point out, "Every courtesy term between persons, every inflection of voice denoting respect or contempt, condescension or dependency, is a statement about the relationship between the two persons" ([1951] 1968, 213). As we speak, we stand at a certain distance, we furrow our brow, and we may use a respectful tone of voice. These nonverbal messages are metacommunicative—they say something about the relationship in which the interaction is taking place. The view of interpersonal communication presented above, in which information (report) and relationship information (command) aspects are contained in every interaction, and where actions convey relationship parameters, has come to be known as the *relational or interactional view of communication.*

INTERPERSONAL COMMUNICATION PATHOLOGIES

The principles of communication described by Ruesch and Bateson, and later by Watzlawick, Beavin Bavelas, and Jackson (1967), were developed primarily as a means to explain why communication becomes pathological. They argue that communication pathologies can be understood as distortions of this relational view of communication. It is driven by the proposition that all behavior in an interaction is communication; that is, every action, whether intended or not, has message value to the other person, even if that action is not to respond. There is no such thing as a "non-behavior" and, as such, there is no such thing as "noncommunication." If I say to you, "the weather is bad" and you say nothing in return, your nonresponse is still a response. It tells me you have not responded, and your message of "I have not responded to you" in turn will generate a response from me, such as "did you hear me?" or "are you upset with me?" or "what are you thinking about?" This means that we can no longer say, as we do within the paradigm of the transmission view, that communication only takes place when it is intentional, conscious, or successful, that is, when we achieve a mutual understanding of some idea I intend to transmit to you. Watzlawick and his colleagues' extension of Ruesch and Bateson's work demonstrates that communication is a function of *our behaviors toward one another,* and not of our psychical states. All behavior is communication (a facial tick, a body movement, a blink of an eye, silence) and not all behavior is necessarily intentional.

One can see how this principle can be distorted to produce potentially pathological behavior. That fact that one must always communicate when in the presence of another (one cannot turn it off, according to Watzlawick, Beavin Bavelas, and Jackson) implies that communication always involves *choices.* It is the choices that we are faced with, and that we must make, that determine the effectiveness of our communication.

Watzlawick, Beavin Bavelas, and Jackson offer the following example, which is adapted to reflect a library context. Consider two strangers, Arthur and Bill, who are assigned adjacent seats on an airplane. Arthur, for whatever reason, does not want to talk to Bill. What can Arthur do to avoid conversation as the long flight inevitably unfolds? As Watzlawick points out, "there are two things [Arthur] cannot do: he cannot physically leave the field [he can't leave the airplane!], and he cannot *not* communicate" (Watzlawick, Beavin Bavelas, and Jackson 1967, 75). Much to Arthur's chagrin, Bill does indeed attempt to strike up a conversation. He says, "Hi, my name is Bill. Where are you going?" Let us consider the options Arthur has in response to Bill in order to further his desire not to talk. As we will see, all of them involve communicating, whether through talk or other means. The first option would be explicit *rejection:* Arthur can simply tell Bill he is not interested in having a conversation. He could say, "Look Bill, you seem a really friendly guy, but I would rather not talk during the flight." This may certainly work to stifle Bill's approaches, but it could also be potentially embarrassing, perhaps even rude, and lead to a strained and uncomfortable atmosphere during the flight. Arthur would like to avoid this if at all possible. For a host of reasons people usually and ritually choose civility above other, possibly unpleasant alternatives. (This will be discussed in those chapters focusing on the work of Erving Goffman).

A second response would be for Arthur to accept Bill's initial offer to converse in the hope that his terse reactions might satisfy Bill that he is not a rude person, but not enough to encourage further conversation. He might say, "Hi Bill. My name is Arthur. I'm off to Chicago." Although this response satisfies Bill's initial question, inevitably it leads to more. Bill says, "Chicago? Great city for sightseeing. What are you doing there?" Arthur is compelled to reply, "I'm not there to see the city [chuckles]. I am attending a professional conference." Again, Bill's question is answered, but Arthur's response only serves to generate another question, "What kind of conference is it? What do you do?" Arthur discloses that he is a librarian heading to Chicago to attend the American Library Association conference, Bill discloses that he is a marketing executive, and the conversation is off and running for another hour, just like our description of Gadamer's "genuine conversation" in chapter 2. This leads to Arthur feeling frustrated, because his attempts to fend off Bill by answering his questions have only led to more questions, and more responses, and more questions, and so on, and all the while Bill is getting more comfortable and familiar, leading to more conversation.

A third option is what Watzlawick terms "disqualification of communication:" Arthur could respond in nonstandard ways. He could say something like, "Why do you want to know where I'm going? What business is it of yours?" Or Arthur could feign sleepiness or some other condition as an excuse not to talk. He could claim to have a headache, or he has to read a report, or he could slip on headphones and listen to an iPod, or bring out a laptop or tablet and work. The point is that Arthur has no choice *but to communicate,* regardless of what he does or does not do. Additionally, the choice Arthur makes also communicates something about his relationship to Bill. He is not communicating about the content of Bill's words, but rather the relationship he wishes to exist, or not exist, between them. In this example, it can be seen that interpersonal communication is not just about transmitting ideas, it is about making choices that serve to establish and maintain relationships between people.

According to Watzlawick and colleagues, recognizing and acknowledging patterns and potential patterns of communication, such as those between Arthur and Bill above, are the focus of therapeutic intervention. To illustrate with another library example, take the case of the head of reference at a public library who discovers (on Friday) that there is no one to staff the desk on Saturday. He quickly calls one of the part-timers to ask if he can cover. When the library director finds out, she is upset because this action has a budget impact and she feels strongly that the head of reference should have consulted her first. The head of reference usually does consult the director, but felt that in this case there was insufficient time. Subsequently they quarrel. Looking back on the interaction, both the director and the head of reference agreed that the decision was perfectly appropriate and that had she been consulted, the director would have agreed to the call. So why did they quarrel? It was as if they both agreed and disagreed about the same issue.

To look a bit deeper, here are two issues to consider in this case. The first is the practical matter of the need to staff the service desk on Saturday. That much the pair agreed on. The second is the matter of the relationship between the head of reference and the library director, and the fact the department head had taken the initiative of calling the part-timer without consulting the director. Making the call was not the issue. The issue was what making the call without budget approval said about the pair's working relationship, and that the library director felt slighted by not being included in a decision that would affect the budget. The issue was the lack of consultation, rather than the act. It was the way the call was made, not the call itself, and what the manner of events said about the department head's attitudes towards the director and his relationship with her. The problem (or pathology, if you will) here is not concerned with the content of the communication (the report dimension), but rather the relationship that this report implied (the command or relational dimension). Indeed, the resolution of content issues may fail to result in the resolution of relational issues. Indeed, it may make them worse.

Consider a situation where a couple is arguing about a question of fact, such as where they went on holiday in 2009. The husband says Florida while the wife says the Jersey Shore. The content issue here is easily resolved by going to the family photo album, and finding out that in 2009, the couple had a lovely week in Belmar, New Jersey. However, the resolution of the content dimension leads to further issues in the relational dimension. If the relationship is a troubled one, the husband may feel humiliated because he was wrong, and resentful that his wife was correct. The wife may feel superior to have put one over on her know-it-all husband, and takes pleasure in gloating and saying "I told you so." Perhaps the conversation went something like this:

Husband: I was just thinking about our trip to Florida in 2009 and . . .

Wife: We didn't go to Florida in 2009, we went to Belmar, New Jersey.

Husband: Now that's ridiculous, you're wrong. I remember very clearly that we went to Florida and rented that house on the beach.

Wife: Yeah, well that happened, but it was another year. Don't you remember that was the year that Randy wandered off when you said you'd watch him and we . . .

Husband: I can't believe you're bringing that up as a part of this simple conversation about when our vacation occurred! And you're wrong on two counts; your sister was supposed to watch him and that was 2007.

Wife: You never remember anything about our lives. I can't believe you don't remember how panicked we were and besides Randy was nine, not seven, which means it was 2009 and I can show you in the photo album. (*Goes and gets photo album and opens it, showing a page to the husband.*) See, I told you so, there we are on the beach in Belmar![1]

In the course of this conversation, the content issue may have been resolved (they did indeed go to Belmar, New Jersey), but the already shaky relationship between the husband and wife has continued to deteriorate, precisely because the content was resolved! Far from solving the argument, determining the location of the 2009 vacation has only served to heighten the tension. Furthermore, the wife's accusation regarding the issue of the husband's role in an incident where their son went missing brought up a perhaps minor, but definitely sore point between them that further erodes trust. The problem, of course, is that finding the answer to this particular content question is not the issue here. Rather, it is *the conversation* in which the answer was obtained, and the manner in which that conversation took place, that served to deepen the tensions this couple experience in their relationship. Second, the couple is unable to recognize that it is their means of communicating, and the relationship it implies, that is at the root of their problems. The couple is more focused on arguing about content issues and establishing who is "right" and who is "wrong," and about relatively minor issues, such as remembering where they went on holiday. It is the task of the psychiatrist to diagnose problems in the way the couple communicates that is at the heart of the relational view, and bringing the couple's communicative practices to their awareness. Watzlawick and colleagues point out that our relationships are only rarely defined deliberately or with full awareness. They note that "the more spontaneous and 'healthy' a relationship, the more the relationship aspect of communication recedes into the background" (Watzlawick, Beavin Bavelas, and Jackson 1967, 52). However, sick or dysfunctional relationships are characterized by a constant struggle about the nature of the relationship, even if the participants do not recognize this. They continue to fight over the "content" of the interaction (i.e., where they went on holiday) when the issue is the relationship each is trying continually to reestablish (or maintain) with the other.

We can see the impact of the relational dimension and its influence on the communication choices we make in the following example from the library context. This scene opens with a library user (Laurie) standing at the circulation desk and handing a book to the assistant (Chris) to check out. Upon trying to check it out, the circulation assistant finds that Laurie has an overdue fine. If a fine is over ten dollars, the library's procedure is to not allow checkouts until the fine is paid.

Chris: I'm sorry, but according to the computer record, you have a fine of $10.50 for overdue materials you returned last week. You must pay the fine before you can check out this item.

Laurie: I don't have any money on me today. Can I pay next time I come in? I really need this item for a deadline I'm working on.

Chris: I'm not able to let you do that, but you can talk to the department head who is in her office if you like.

Laurie: Ok, that would be good. Thanks.

Chris then goes and gets the department head (Jessica) who is in the middle of doing a report and is annoyed at being interrupted. With a loud sigh, Jessica unhappily gets up and goes with the assistant to the circulation desk.

Jessica (*speaking loudly to Chris in front of Laurie*): "Why are you bothering me with this type of thing? It is only fifty cents over the ten dollar limit. Go ahead and do the override and don't ever bother me again with this type of problem—you already know what to do, just do it!"

Jessica then goes back to the office and shuts the door. Chris turns red, looks down and does the checkout. He is upset for the rest of the day. Laurie also turns red, accepts the book, and mumbles "thanks." She walks away, feeling upset about the interaction she had witnessed, and perhaps that she caused his boss to speak so sharply to Chris.

This exchange between department head (Jessica) and the circulation assistant (Chris) would immediately be recognized as an example of poor interpersonal communication choices by the manager (Jessica); we are now in a position to recognize why this is so, by looking at the interaction from both a content and a relational perspective. On the content level, what Jessica has to say to Chris is certainly clear. She has told the assistant that he is empowered to make these decisions on his own, both in this case and in future cases. The library user, (Laurie) has gotten what she wants, to check out the needed item despite her overdue fine. At the level of content, the interaction can be considered effective and successful.

However, on the relational level, Jessica has made several poor choices in her communication behavior. First of all, she has shamed and embarrassed Chris and Laurie by being condescending and abrupt. Second, she has not thought about what long-term impact this interaction might have on the relationship between her and Chris, or on Laurie's view of the library. Third, Jessica has humiliated Chris in public, in front of Laurie and, indeed, anyone else who might have been near the circulation desk, whether other users, staff, or even possibly upper management. From a relational point of view, this incident will not be quickly forgotten (if at all!) by Chris, even if Jessica chooses to apologize later. Laurie was also shamed by this encounter (because Chris, Jessica, and any others who witnessed this exchange are now aware that a fine was owed and that she did not have the money to pay it, plus she may feel badly that she caused Chris to be reprimanded). The user could potentially have a long-term association with these negative feelings when visiting the library in the future (see also Chelton 1997; Radford and Connaway 2007; Radford 1999, 1993, 2013).

The takeaway from this scenario is to consider carefully the relational dimension of communication in all communication situations, especially ones that are potentially embarrassing to participants. Even though content was successfully communicated (how to deal with a fine of $10.50), relational damage (the embarrassment of both Chris and Laurie) has been done that is likely to be irreparable and long-lasting. Trust has also been compromised.

Consider a more empathetic approach in which the manager takes the relational aspect into account, which could involve two very different conversations: the first in Jessica's office and the second at the circulation desk. Imagine the same scenario as above, taken from the point where Chris goes and talks to Jessica, who is in the middle of working on a report and is annoyed at being interrupted.

Jessica stays seated in her office. She listens to what Chris has to say and replies in a pleasant voice.

Jessica: I'm glad that you brought this to my attention, Chris. I'm tied up here with this report. What do you think? Would it be possible for you to go ahead and do the override, and ask them to come in and pay the fine soon?

Chris: Yes, that sounds good.

Jessica: Okay then, good. I'd also like you to know, by the way, that the next time this type of thing happens, you don't have to ask me. I trust you to use your own judgment, I'm sure you'll know what to do. Thanks.

Consider another alternative situation in which Jessica chooses to get up from working on her report and goes with Chris to the circulation desk.

Jessica greets Laurie with a smile.

Jessica: Hello. Chris here has told me about your fine. Although our policy is to not to allow borrowing if you have more than ten dollars in fines, as Chris has said, in this case, since you are only fifty cents over, we are willing to do the checkout, if you agree to come in soon to pay the fine. I think this will be okay with Chris. (*Turns to Chris and nicely asks*) What do you think?
Chris: Yes, sounds fine. (*Chris checks out the item, and gives eye contact and a pleasant nod to Laurie.*)
Laurie: Thanks so much, I will stop by soon to pay the fine. I really appreciate it.

Soon afterwards Jessica calls Chris in to the office.

Jessica: I am so glad that you brought that overdue fine situation to my attention, thanks. By the way, the next time this happens, I want you to know that you don't have to ask me. I trust you to use your own judgment, I'm sure you'll know what to do. Are you okay with this?

The conversations in these last two scenarios are sensitive to both the content and relational dimensions of communication. They allow Chris to feel like he did the right thing and is empowered to make decisions in the future. The second conversation is also positive, because it reaffirms Chris's self-esteem in front of Laurie by including Chris in the decision to allow the override. The assistant will feel good about the incident and will also know what to do in similar situations in the future. Jessica, as manager, has worked to save the subordinate's face and to involve him in the decision making. In addition, the subordinate has been thanked and praised, which should allow him to feel valued and empowered for the future.

Face-to-face (FtF) conversations are thus revealed to be much more complex and fraught with opportunities to spoil or damage a relationship than we may realize. Situation and context also play a role, as when there are uneven power dynamics (as in boss-subordinate relationships) or in risky conversations where there is a chance of hurting people's feelings or shaming them (as in the overdue fine example), by adding additional factors that influence behaviors (Dainton and Zelley 2011). To add another layer of complexity, think about different modes of communication, including phone or virtual communication (e-mail, texting, or chat), which may be missing the nonverbal cues of a smile or a playful tone, or might involve a queue of users waiting for your attention. A busy physical or virtual reference desk may add stress, anxiety, or a time constraint that is creating a distraction, or requires you to get off the phone, or to end an IM or live chat session that another is eager to continue (see also Burns and Bossaller 2012).

This distinction between content and relationship is important to understanding why certain professional communication situations are "difficult" and others are "easy." In the difficult situations, we are aware that there is more than the content of the message at stake. We know that we wish to establish a particular relationship between ourselves and those we manage, or those to whom we report. We may have the skills and confidence to manage what we say, but have far less confidence that we know how to manage the relationships that our communication choices will inevitably create. Chapter 4 will build upon these basic principles of the interactional approach to communication, providing more depth to our understanding of communication as it is manifest in behavior.

REFERENCES

Burns, C. Sean, and Jenny Bossaller. 2012. "Communication Overload: A Phenomenological Inquiry into Academic Reference Librarianship." *Journal of Documentation,* 68 (5): 597–617.

Carey, James. 1992. *Communication as Culture.* New York: Routledge.

Chelton, Mary K. 1997. "The 'Overdue Kid': A Face-to-Face Library Service Encounter as Ritual Interaction." *Library and Information Science Research* 9 (4): 387–99.

Dainton, Marianne, and Elaine D. Zelley. 2011. *Applying Communication Theory for Professional Life: A Practical Introduction,* 2nd edition. Los Angeles: Sage.

Fine, Sara. 1995. "Reference and Resources: The Human Side." *The Journal of Academic Librarianship* 21 (1): 17–20.

Habermas, Jürgen. 1990. *Moral Consciousness and Communicative Action.* Translated by Christian Lenhardt and Shierry Weber Nicholsen. Cambridge, MA: MIT Press.

Locke, John. 1690/1975. *An Essay Concerning Human Understanding,* edited by Peter H. Nidditch. Oxford, UK: Clarendon Press.

Menninger, Roy W., and John C. Nemiah, eds. 2000. *American Psychiatry after World War II, 1944–1994.* Washington, DC: American Psychiatric Press.

Oxford English Dictionary. 2015. "Communication, N." *OED Online.* October 2015. Oxford University Press. Available: www.oed.com/.

Pearce, Barnett. 1994. *Interpersonal Communication: Making Social Worlds.* New York: Harper Collins.

Radford, Gary P., and Marie L. Radford. 2005. "Structuralism, Post-Structuralism, and the Library: de Saussure and Foucault." *Journal of Documentation* 51 (1): 60–78.

Radford, Marie L. 2013. "Rethinking Interpersonal Communication for Managers." In *Managing in the Middle,* edited by Robert Farrell and Kenneth Schlesinger, 33–37, Chicago: ALA Editions.

———. 1999. *The Reference Encounter: Interpersonal Communication in the Academic Library.* Chicago: Association of College and Research Libraries.

———. 1993. "Relational Aspects of Reference Interactions: A Qualitative Investigation of the Perceptions of Users and Librarians in the Academic Library." PhD diss., Rutgers, The State University of New Jersey.

Radford, Marie L., and Lynn S. Connaway. 2007. "'Screenagers' and Live Chat Reference: Living Up to the Promise." *Scan* 26 (1): 31–39.

Ruesch, Jurgen, and Gregory Bateson. 1968. *Communication: The Social Matrix of Psychiatry.* New York: Norton.

Shannon, Claude, and Warren Weaver. 1949. *The Mathematical Theory of Communication.* Urbana, IL: University of Illinois Press.

Warnke, Georgia. 1995. "Communicative Rationality and Cultural Values." In *The Cambridge Companion to Habermas,* edited by Stephen K. White, 120–42. Cambridge, UK: Cambridge University Press.

Watzlawick, Paul, Janet Beavin Bavelas, and Don D. Jackson. 1967. *Pragmatics of Human Communication.* New York: Norton.

NOTE

1. The authors wish to thank Stefani Gomez for suggesting the idea for this example.

An Interactional View of Interpersonal Communication

Reclaiming Watzlawick, Beavin Bavelas, and Jackson's *Pragmatics of Human Communication*

We are in constant communication, and yet we are almost completely unable to communicate about communication.

—WATZLAWICK, BEAVIN BAVELAS, AND JACKSON (1967, 36)

I t seems normal for us to view our interpersonal communication behavior as a function of ourselves as individuals. When we talk, text, or chat online with another person, we consider what we do and what we say to be an expression of *us,* of who we are, and what we are thinking and feeling. In our American culture, we are encouraged to speak our mind, and say what we feel. It seems natural to suppose that the act of communication begins inside of us (an idea, thought, or emotion is created within our mind), and our communication behavior enables us to get outside what otherwise would remain inside us. As introduced in chapter 3, the relational approach to interpersonal communication holds the view that the major concern is *not* what happens within people's heads or minds, nor the psychological or mental processes by which an idea might be formed in either the mind of a person sending that idea or of the mind of the person receiving it. Rather, interpersonal communication is viewed from the standpoint of behavior. It is not what or how people *think* that is important, rather it is what people *do*. Watzlawick, Beavin Bavelas, and Jackson (1967) refer to the relationship of communication and behavior as the *pragmatics of human communication* or the *interactional view,* and that is the view we wish to reclaim in this chapter.

The foundation of an interactional view of interpersonal communication is the recognition that all acts of communication (whether face-to-face [FtF] or virtual) are acts of behavior. We perform acts of speaking. Verbal communication is something we do. That much would seem obvious. However, Watzlawick, Beavin Bavelas, and Jackson make the claim that all acts of behavior are also acts of communication. It is not just the words we say in a conversation that are important, but also the ways in which those words are said. We may accompany our speech act with a smile, a nod of the head, a gesture, or in virtual realms with an "LOL," smiley emoticon, or emoji. We may look into the other person's eyes or look away. We may stand close to that person or at a distance. We may raise our voice or speak in a whisper. We may type in all caps for emphasis or to express annoyance. These are all behaviors that occur in the act of communication, but they are all behaviors that have information value. In a conversation, we may wonder: Why is the person looking at me so intently? Why are they talking so softly? Why are they smiling as they speak? What did they mean by typing "LOL" in a serious chat conversation about a new hire? We quickly and intuitively try to make some sense of these behaviors, to guess at their meanings. In a conversation, trying to make the distinction between behavior and communication becomes difficult, if not impossible, because our acts of communication *are* behaviors. A conversation is a sequence of behaviors between two or more people. Who is to say which behaviors in these sequences are not communicative: the glance at a watch, the raising of an eyebrow, the slight lean forward, and the lilting rise in the volume at the end of a sentence, a misspelled word or inappropriate grammar in a virtual reference session? Indeed, is there *any* behavior that cannot be considered to be meaningful, even when it is not intended by the speaker?

RESPONDING TO OTHERS

The fact that people respond to each other's behavior in a conversation in unpredictable and unique ways is key to the interactional view of interpersonal communication. Unlike a strategic approach to interpersonal communication, which is concerned with what effects a communication/behavior has on another person, an interactional focus also takes into account the effect that the receiver's response has on the sender. For example, in a conversation you have with your colleague Anne, not only is your behavior being interpreted and acted upon by Anne, but you are also interpreting and acting upon Anne's behavior. The focus of this way of thinking about communication is not on the relationship of the receiver with *the message* (that is, how did the receiver understand what is said), but rather on the *relationship between the sender and the receiver as it is mediated by communication/behavior.* This is a fundamental distinction that will be a major emphasis of the interactional approach. We are not concerned with what happens in a perceiver's mind (how they understand, how they perceive), but rather with what they do, how they react, how they behave, and how this behavior forms the frame that will determine how both people in conversation will act.

Watzlawick, Beavin Bavelas, and Jackson (1967) offered the following model to articulate these dynamics:

FIGURE 4.1

Interaction Model

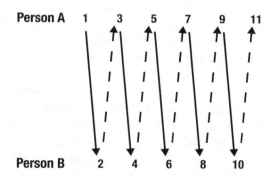

Adapted from Watzlawick, Beavin Bavelas, and Jackson, 1967.

As shown in figure 4.1, the Interaction Model depicts a conversation between person A and person B in which person A sends a message to person B (solid line), which creates a response from person B (dotted line). Person B's response then acts as a message to person A, which in turn produces a response from person A. The key insight is that any utterance in this model, for example the message from A to B at point 5, is *both* a message to B *and* a response to B. The communication behavior of A makes possible the communication behavior of B. However, the same communication behavior of B makes possible the communication behavior of A. A's communication behavior at point 5 in this interaction is made possible by the interaction pattern of messages and responses that came before it, and that same behavior will become part of the same ongoing interaction pattern that will make possible the communication behaviors at points 6, 7, and beyond. Without A's action at point 5, the behaviors at points 6 and 7 would not come to exist in the way they did. Instead, something different would be said or done, depending what happened at point 5.

We can demonstrate this model with a simple exercise. Sit or stand directly opposite a partner. Hold up your hands so that your palms are directly facing the palms of your partner. Do not let your palms touch. Slowly begin moving both arms in large circles, always keeping your palms facing those of your partner. Make sure your movements are smooth and languid so your palms are always keep together (remember, without touching). As the circle motion becomes established, and you feel comfortable that your palms will not stray away from the palms of your partner, begin to move your arms in different and more spontaneous directions. Your partner should shift the position of her palms so they remain opposite yours as you smoothly shift direction. At the same time, you should shift the movement of your palms in response to any new movement by your partner.

This exercise is a physical equivalent of Escher's *Drawing Hands* sketch (see figure 3.1), in which the action of the first hand makes possible the action of the second, and the action of the second hand makes possible the action of first. Every movement of your hand is a message to be responded to; that is, when your hand moves, your partner is compelled to follow. However, should your partner's hand stop, or move in another direction, you are compelled to respond to your partner's behavior. In other words, every movement of your hand is *both* a movement to be followed *and* a movement that is following the hand of the other. If you do this exercise without a prior agreement that one of you will lead and the other will follow, you will find that identifying the person in charge of the movement is impossible. You may certainly choose to move your hand any way you wish, but if your partner's hand does not follow and moves somewhere else, you will find that you are compelled to follow the movement of your partner. If you do not, then you cannot carry on the exercise. You will find that the ability to move your hand is contingent on the movement of your partner and, at the same time, the movement of your partner is contingent on you.

A person observing the movement of your hands could describe the pattern of your movements: of how your hands moved upwards, then down, then in a circle, then back and forth, and so on. This person would be describing an *interaction pattern,* the pattern produced as a result of you and your partner coming together and moving your hands in unison. The pattern is not your creation alone, nor is it the creation of your partner alone. The pattern only comes into being when you and your partner act together such that your movement is contingent upon her movement, and her movement is contingent upon your movement. The movement of one individual cannot control the creation and shape of the pattern. Indeed, it is the pattern that determines where your hands can move. One cannot predict what your hands will be doing just a few seconds from now. You may be making circles, or you may be making straight lines. You will not know what you will be doing until the pattern reaches that point in time. You can certainly try and control the pattern, and attempt to force your partner to move where you want. But you will find that your ability to control the pattern is completely dependent on the cooperation of your partner, and any movement that deviates from yours will compel you to break away from your individual objectives and follow the other; otherwise, the pattern will collapse completely.

A conversation is an interaction pattern in exactly the same way as the pattern produced in the movement of your hands. What you say and do in a conversation is contingent upon what the other person is saying and doing, and what the other person is saying and doing is contingent upon what you are saying and doing. The sequence of messages passing back and forth between the participants creates an interaction pattern that cannot be controlled by either person. What is said and done at any particular point in the conversation is dependent upon its place in the interaction pattern, and what the context of the pattern will allow as appropriate. Any attempts to forcibly control the interaction will inevitably lead to the conversation breaking down.

Watzlawick's model makes it clear that in an interactional view, the distinction between a "sender" and a "receiver" dissolves and disappears. The act of sending a message is simultaneously also a response to what the other person has just said or done. At the same time, the act of responding to a message is simultaneously sending a message to the other person. To take a very simple example: one morning I see you on a sidewalk near the library and say "hello." It could be said that by saying "hello," I am acting as a sender and sending you a message. But ask yourself why I am saying this? This act did not come out of thin air. Obviously, I saw you. I became aware of your presence. Perhaps you looked at me and we established eye contact, however brief. I became aware that you were aware of my presence. As a result of these behaviors, all with information value to me, I say "hello" to you. So not only is my greeting a message sent to you, it is also a response to your behaviors that nonverbally invite me to speak. The greeting "hello" is simultaneously a message and a response. Your behavior made my utterance possible. Similarly, my greeting of "hello" makes possible an utterance from you. You say "hello" in return. Now your "hello" is both a response to my greeting, and a message to me that my greeting has been acknowledged and the floor is now open to say something else. As with Escher's *Drawing Hands,* your behavior makes possible my greeting, and my greeting makes possible your behavior. We both provide the conditions in which any further conversation will make sense.

Let us consider these concepts in the context of a longer conversation. The following conversation is taken from the opening chapter of Raymond Chandler's novel *The Little Sister* (1949, 5–6), and represents a service encounter of a fictional kind between a client and a service provider. Like many conversations in the library, it takes place between strangers and is goal-directed. We will examine how the words uttered by one person make possible the words that the other says, and how the sequence of these spoken words produces a pattern in which any given utterance comes to make sense. The point we wish to make is that the meaning or significance of any particular words should not be found in the individual's understanding or intentions, but rather in the place it appears in the conversational pattern. Read the following conversation between private eye Phillip Marlowe and a potential client. Look at how it flows, back and forth, and settles into a rhythm that is created neither by Marlowe nor his potential client, but rather by the two of them working together, exchanging words back and forth, to the point where what is said at any time derives from the rhythm of the conversation, rather than any particular objective of each person.

The scene begins with hard-boiled detective Marlowe idling away the time stalking a bluebottle fly with a swatter in his office. The phone rings, and Marlowe is greeted by a "small, rather hurried, little-girlish voice," which asks how much he charges for his services. Marlowe quotes his fee of "forty bucks a day and expenses." The little voice balks: "That's far too much . . . Why, it might cost hundreds of dollars and I only get a small salary and—." Marlowe cuts the voice off at this point and asks the woman from where she is calling. She reveals that she is in the drugstore in the building next to his office. Marlowe quips, "You could have saved a nickel. The elevator's free." The woman is taken aback at Marlowe's informality. Marlowe realizes this and takes a more patient and empathetic tone. He invites her to his office and adds, "If you're in my kind of trouble, I can give you a pretty good idea." The conversation continues:

> "I have to know something about you," the small voice said very firmly.
> "This is a very delicate matter, very personal. I couldn't talk to just anybody."

"If it's that delicate," I said, "maybe you need a lady detective."

"Goodness, I didn't know there were any." Pause. "But I don't think a lady detective would do at all. You see, Orrin was living in a very tough neighborhood, Mr. Marlowe. At least I thought it was tough. The manager of the rooming house is a most unpleasant person. He smelled of liquor. Do you drink, Mr. Marlowe?"

"Well, now that you mention it—"

"I don't think I'd care to employ a detective that uses liquor in any form. I don't even approve of tobacco."

"Would it be all right if I peeled an orange?"

I caught the sharp intake of breath at the far end of the line. "You might at least talk like a gentleman," she said.

The interactional view of interpersonal communication claims that what is said at any given point in the conversation is rendered meaningful by its place in the interaction pattern, rather than any specific objective intended by the speaker. To demonstrate this claim, we will consider Marlowe's words: "If it's that delicate, maybe you need a lady detective."

Consider why Marlowe said this and what it means in the context of this conversation. One might say that Marlowe has the intention of recommending a "lady detective" to his client, and so makes this statement to achieve this goal. Perhaps Marlowe intends to make a joke, and make his client feel at ease. Or perhaps Marlowe is frustrated by the client and makes this assertion to belittle her. In the context of the conversation, what Marlowe individually means or intends is not the driving force of the spoken message. That message was not initiated by a thought in Marlowe's head that he then acted to express. The phrase "If it's that delicate, maybe you need a lady detective" is a response to the client's declaration that preceded it, where she said: "I have to know something about you. This is a very delicate matter, very personal. I couldn't talk to just anybody." Marlowe's statement is building upon and responding to the client's use of terms such as "delicate" and "personal." If the client had not used these particular terms, then Marlowe's quip about the "lady detective" would not have appeared and Marlowe would have said something else. Marlowe's statement is made meaningful by the context of the declaration to which it is a response.

When this particular conversation started, neither Marlowe nor his client could have predicted that just a few seconds into the conversation, the phrase "maybe you need a lady detective" would have appeared. That is because at any point in the conversation, there is really no way of knowing what will be said, even a few conversational turns into the future. Marlowe's quip about the lady detective was made possible by the conversational flow itself. It just "seemed right" to make this quip at this point in the conversation, and it could only be made once the client had offered Marlowe the conversational opening by using the terms "delicate" and "personal." In other words, the lady detective quip was spontaneous, rather than planned, and it came as a response to a statement that was itself spontaneous.

Indeed, the client's utterance about her concern being "a very delicate matter, very personal" was made as a response to Marlowe inviting her up to his office and saying "If you're in my kind of trouble, I can give you a pretty good idea." So Marlowe's quip about the lady detective was produced as a spontaneous reaction to the client's use of "delicate" and "personal" which themselves were a spontaneous response to Marlowe's "Come on up and let's have a look at you. If you're in my kind of trouble, I can give you a pretty good idea." and so on. The critical point is that neither Marlowe nor his client is controlling this conversation. Both certainly have objectives they would like to achieve through the conversation: the client wishes to find a detective to take her delicate and personal case, and Marlowe is interested in gaining a new client. But neither of the participants is able to control the flow of the conversation in any direct manner, and in the end, neither achieve their objective, at least at this point in Chandler's story. In any conversation, what is said by one person elicits a reaction from the other person. However, that reaction determines a reaction from the first person, and so it goes.

As Watzlawick and colleagues describe, "whatever B does influences A's next move, and . . . they are both largely influenced by, and in turn influence, the context in which that interaction takes place" (Watzlawick, Beavin Bavelas, and Jackson 1967, 36). The participants will know more than a little about the interaction beforehand, even before the first words are spoken. When the client calls Marlowe's office, she will have a good idea of the kind of conversation that is about to take place. She will expect to participate in a conversation that would be appropriate between a client and a potential service provider. She will expect to discuss fees, availability, and, in this case, the suitability of Marlowe to handle her case. These expectations enable the participants to recognize inconsistencies or behavior that seem out of context. However, the actual words and sentences that will make up the conversation (and the eventual outcome) will be unknown until they actually come into existence.

This is because the emergence of each conversational turn is dependent upon what dialog has preceded it, and future utterances are dependent upon what has just been said. For example, at the end of the conversation, Marlowe asks, "Would it be all right if I peeled an orange?" Neither Marlowe nor the client could have predicted that this question would have been asked prior to the start of this conversation. The client could not have planned to say anything that would have provoked Marlowe to ask this question. Marlowe could not have predicted that the client would have made a statement that would have *allowed* him to ask this question and have it make sense. It feels strange to hear the question, "would it be all right if I peeled an orange?" in what is essentially a service encounter, but in the context of this particular conversation, and the pattern of previous conversation that has come before, it makes perfect sense. So the question, "would it be all right if I peeled an orange?" seems to break the rules of a service encounter, and yet it follows the rules that have been established in this particular conversation. In one context, the question seems entirely inappropriate and yet, in another context, becomes entirely appropriate.

The ambiguity of appropriateness is key to understanding conversations in the interactional perspective. We do not necessarily know which rules are being followed in a successful conversation, and which rules are being broken in an unsuccessful conversation. We seem to know the rules without knowing them, or sometimes the rules seem to be created as we go along. And this seems to be the reason we need so many workshops, courses, seminars, and self-help books about communication. Despite all of our knowledge of conversational tips and tactics, the spontaneous and unpredictable nature of interactions means that control (and perhaps understanding) of what is going on at any given moment remains tantalizingly outside of our grasp. As Watzlawick and his colleagues put it, "We are in constant communication, and yet we are almost completely unable to communicate about communication" (Watzlawick, Beavin Bavelas, and Jackson 1967, 36).

Consider this example of the interactional view occurring in a library environment. Danny has just started a job as the director of a medium-sized college library. She realizes that she must work to become acclimated to the library culture and build positive relationships with her staff to be an effective leader. She decides that a good way to start to get to know her subordinates is to meet with them individually. She decides to focus these meetings on staff professional goals and getting some suggestions for which priorities she should consider most important. With a positive spirit and warm feelings toward her new colleagues, she starts with one of the department heads, Paulette.

Danny: "Hi Paulette, thanks for coming in today. I'm meeting with everyone as I'm starting to settle in as director, and you are the first! I'd like to ask for your help in getting to know you better, to learn about your professional goals and also in hearing your suggestions for top organizational priorities for me to address."

Paulette *(takes a deep breath and leans forward)*: "Sure, but before we get started, I've come to bring a problem to your attention, one that has been getting worse and needs immediate action."

Danny *(somewhat startled)*: "Oh . . . okay, talk to me, what is it?"

Paulette: "I'm very frustrated and hope you can help. One of the librarians I supervise, Erin, has a chronic problem with low productivity. For example, she's not holding up her end of a weeding project. In fact, I think she's just reading in the stacks instead of identifying damaged or outdated books to be discarded. We are short on space and this project is a priority. Her lack of progress has been apparent to me for weeks. I'd like you to address this problem immediately as I've gotten nowhere when I talk to her."

Danny *(with an inward sigh)*: "I'd like to help resolve this problem. Tell me more about Erin and what you have already done."

Paulette *(becoming agitated)*: "Oh, I've just tried everything. I'm out of patience. You have to do something now! The previous director just looked the other way!"

In this example, Danny begins the conversation with a particular goal in mind; she wants to get to know Paulette. But notice how the conversation develops to derail this initial goal very quickly—indeed, in Paulette's very first response to Danny's opening remarks. Paulette has a problem she has been unable to solve and presents a challenge to Danny in demanding immediate action. Once Paulette brings up this problem in the conversation, Danny cannot simply brush away Paulette's concern and continue with her own agenda without consequence. Instead, Paulette's response leads Danny to ask, "What is it?" From there the conversation takes on an entirely new direction, and Danny responds by taking an appropriate role in this new flow.

From a strategic point of view, it might be said that Danny's conversational skills were deficient, and her attempts to get to know Paulette were a failure. We might say that Danny's preferred conversation has been hijacked and her agenda has been replaced by Paulette's agenda. That is certainly one way we could look at this conversation. But let's consider what might have happened if Danny had attempted to assert control of the conversation such that it returned to serve her agenda. What could Danny have said to achieve this? Paulette's utterance in response to Danny's opening was, "Sure, but before we get started, I've come to bring a problem to your attention, one that has been getting worse and needs immediate action." Remember, in the interactional view, every utterance is both a response to the other, and a message to the other. So Paulette's statement is a response to Danny's utterance, and a message to Danny that itself demands a response. It would be difficult for Danny to ignore Paulette's statement or pretend it did not happen. In this particular scenario, she really cannot continue as if Paulette had said nothing. The conversation compels Danny to respond to Paulette's response/message. So Danny replies, as indeed she is arguably compelled to do here: "Oh . . . okay, talk to me, what is it?"

The important insight of the interactional view is that in a conversation such as this one, there is no right or wrong way to behave, or a right or wrong thing to say. In a conversation, one must consider the *appropriate* thing to say, given the context of the conversation taking place. One cannot judge Danny's response of "talk to me, what is it?" in terms of correctness, or effectiveness. But one can say Danny's response was appropriate. After all, in Danny's position as the new director, and Paulette's position as a department head, although Danny has a choice of what words to say, the essence of her response has to be to ask Paulette to elaborate on her problem. What else could Danny have said without coming across as dismissive, insensitive, or even rude?

Let's suppose that Danny did not respond directly to Paulette's concern and instead replied with a statement intended to pursue her own objectives. So, instead of responding with "Oh . . . okay, talk to me, what is it?" what if Danny had said: "Yes, sure, we can talk about that later. At the moment, I want to focus on what initiatives you are pursuing in your department." This certainly would have furthered Danny's individual goals, but what message would this send to Paulette? Would Paulette feel slighted, or assume that her concerns were unimportant? And what might be the consequences of this perception for future interactions? Little exchanges such as this may seem trivial at the time, and yet they have the potential to shape and color interactions in the future for perhaps years to come.

To take this example one step further, what possible responses would Paulette have had if Danny had tried to put off the conversation about the unproductive librarian that Paulette wanted to pursue? Paulette would then have been put in the position of having to make a choice. She could continue to pursue her own concerns about the progress of the important weeding project. However, this time she would do this in the knowledge that her first attempt to raise the subject was not acknowledged, and there remains the possibility that a second initiation might lead to further rejection. Perhaps this fear would lead Paulette not to raise the issue directly, because she now believes that Danny is not interested in this problem, or perhaps she imagines that Danny thinks this is a problem for Paulette, and not for a library director. Therefore, another option for Paulette would be to follow Danny's conversational lead and continue to talk about her department and her goals, and let the problem-employee subject drop altogether. By not responding to Paulette's concern, Danny has certainly steered this particular conversation in the direction she wanted (she has compelled Paulette to discuss her department), and, from a strategic point of view, we might say that Danny's conversational skills have been successful and effective. However, this single response will also lay the groundwork for conversations that will occur in the future, which may be tinged by feelings of resentment in Paulette that were seeded in that one single exchange that is taking place in their initial, formative meeting. In that respect, Danny's strategic moves in this conversation may lead to more problematic conversations in the future.

The principle that guides our discussion of interpersonal communication, then, is not effectiveness or correctness, but rather how to communicate *wisely*. Good interpersonal communicators recognize that conversations are inherently dynamic, fluid, spontaneous, and unpredictable. One never knows what will happen next, or when one's feelings will get hurt, or when an exchange will lead to an idea that neither participant would have dreamed of just five minutes earlier. Interpersonal communication in the professional setting entails more than achieving results, or getting our way. It is about having the ability to recognize critical moments in a conversation, and making good decisions about how to proceed appropriately.

Simply put, interpersonal communication is not about getting the other person to do what you want, to "get with the program." It is about thoughtfully and usefully understanding and guiding action that is constantly happening in the real world. The appropriate metaphor would be guiding a small boat through rough seas, where the skilled sailor responds to the push of each oncoming wave and each burst of wind, coordinating her actions skillfully with the actions of the environment in which she finds herself. To succeed, she must work with the environment, and make her actions part of its actions. A conversation represents a similar kind of environment. It is a context that must be travelled and negotiated with a constant sensitivity to the ebbs and flows of the interaction, and where one must constantly adjust one's communication behaviors to successfully make that journey.

Unfortunately, there is no system of tips or strategies that will work in every conceivable interpersonal communication situation. There is no "one size fits all" when it comes to conversations. But this is not a shortcoming of the interactional approach. Indeed, it is a key realization because, without it, people will believe there is a "right way to communicate" and that there are universal modes of effective communication behaviors, if only we could identify and practice them. The insight that such behaviors do not exist is crucial when approaching interpersonal communication in the professional setting. The key realization is not that we need to know how to communicate *correctly,* but rather that we need to know how to communicate *wisely* and *usefully* in the context of relationships and situations that are fluid and constantly changing.

The goal of the successful communicator is not to deploy the correct behavior at the right time, but rather to be able to identify critical moments in an interaction and to act appropriately and thoughtfully in response to them. The reality is that interpersonal communication situations faced by professionals are not only problems to be solved on a content level. We must realize that conversations are also sites of potentially critical communication that have the potential to change the perceptions, relationships, and future conversations of the participants for a long time to come. Faced with this, when the manager Danny meets with Paulette, she is not merely considering the question of, "what is the correct thing to do here?" as if there were a single correct course of action to take. Rather, Danny should ask, "what is the wise thing to do here?" (Pearce 2008). For all of us, our awareness of the potential outcomes of conversational actions we decide to take become critically important in professional situations. Although Danny has specific goals for this meeting, she can nonetheless have the wise insight that she is in no position to completely control the outcomes of this conversation with Paulette. No matter what Danny's intentions are, the conversation can turn on the choice of a word, the look on a face, or an event totally outside of her control. Communication behavior that the manager considers to be friendly and helpful might be interpreted by the employee as condescending and patronizing.

So, although it may be impossible to do the correct thing, it is possible to do the wise thing, just as Aristotle said in his discussion of phronesis many centuries ago. Danny needs to understand that what is at stake is not her personal characteristics, that is, her personal honesty or integrity. Nor is it about the effect of one act with one outcome. The conversation is not about the effect of particular actions. Interpersonal communication is a continuing process of action and reflection. What takes place in this one conversation will have implications and consequences far beyond that particular situation. Danny's decision to abandon her immediate plan (to discover staff professional goals and to get suggestions for staff views of her top priorities), and to respond by asking "Oh . . . okay, talk to me, what is it?" is appropriate and wise in this situation. Danny's future relationship with Paulette (and

Paulette's relationship with Danny) is being mutually created within their conversation—as in Escher's sketch of *Drawing Hands* (discussed in chapter 3; see figure 3.1)—and will have direct influence upon all their future encounters.

REFERENCES

Chandler, Raymond. 1949. *The Little Sister.* London: Pan Books.

Pearce, W. Barnett. 2008. "Toward a New Repertoire of Communication Skills for Leaders and Managers." *The Quality Management Forum* 34 (4): 4–7.

Watzlawick, Paul, Janet B. Beavin Bavelas, and Don D. Jackson. 1967. *Pragmatics of Human Communication.* New York: Norton.

PART 2

Applying Theory to Reference Encounters

Interpersonal Communication as Face-Work within Reference Encounters

Reclaiming Erving Goffman's "On Face-Work"

Much of the activity occurring during an encounter can be understood as an effort on everyone's part to get through the occasion and all the unanticipated and unintentional events that can cast participants in an undesirable light, without disrupting the relationships of the participants.

—ERVING GOFFMAN (1967, 41)

P revious chapters in part 1 of this book have introduced the idea of relational communication and the ways in which interpersonal encounters enable conversations to be co-constructed by individuals. Part 2 applies the ideas of relational communication and related theories to a specific context within libraries, the reference service encounter, including both face-to-face (FtF) and virtual, and presents a relational model of success in chapter 6.

In this chapter, we build upon what was previously discussed by considering the insightful thoughts of the late sociologist Erving Goffman, and applying these to reference interactions. Goffman studied the behavior of ordinary people, and wrote extensively about how we engage with others in rituals that structure encounters and enable us to get through day-to-day conversations without disrupting our relationships. This chapter introduces a powerful example to illustrate Goffman's concepts through a detailed discussion of a live chat reference encounter that soon becomes sour and eventually ends in a reference disaster.

Goffman (1959, 1964, 1967) emphasizes *context* as one of the most essential components of how individuals construct meanings in conversations. Conversations do not exist in a vacuum, but rather are always framed within social situations, including professional situations like those occurring in and about libraries. Goffman defines a social situation as "an environment of mutual monitoring possibilities anywhere within which an individual will find himself accessible to the naked senses of all others who are 'present' and similarly find themselves accessible to him" (Goffman 1964, 63).

This environment of mutual monitoring encompasses all of the behaviors in a conversation, not just the words that are spoken. So all of the nonverbal behaviors available to our senses are involved: sight, sound, touch, smell, and taste. These include facial expressions, posture and the way we walk, eye contact, tone of voice, gesture, interpersonal distance, and physical contact (e.g., a handshake). The difference between *what is said* and *how it is said* is a main focus of strategic approaches to interpersonal communication, as discussed throughout this book. We are inundated with advice on how to manipulate how we say things (e.g., speak in a positive tone, have a firm handshake, look your conversational partner in the eye) in the belief that controlling how we act can somehow shape the outcome of a conversation in our favor. However, any and all behaviors in the "environment of mutual monitoring possibilities" of a given conversation have the potential to prompt certain reactions from another person that make such direct control quite impossible (Manusov and Patterson 2006). If you consider the sheer number of nonverbal behaviors and cues that are being given off by people in any interpersonal encounter, then it is not surprising that the idea of controlling all of this behavior becomes unrealistic. Not only is it very difficult to control every aspect of our own behavior, it is also impossible to predict which particular behaviors and cues will be responded to by other people at any particular moment. You may take great pains to speak in a confident and assertive manner, and shake hands with a firm grip, but all that the other person might notice is your new designer eyeglasses, or the interesting way your hair falls over your left eye.

Goffman recognizes that conversations are inherently risky, because every time we talk (or virtually interact) with someone there is a possibility of jeopardizing a budding or continuing relationship. Who knows what we might say or do at any moment that will send our conversational partner down the wrong track? For example, you might inadvertently frown during the course of a conversation. How does the other person you are talking to interpret the frown? He would have to look at what's been happening in the course of an ongoing sequence of interactions. Were you discussing a budget cut, or a staff member that needed to be given closer supervision, or a scheduling conflict?

Given the uncertainty and unpredictability inherent in all conversations, Goffman famously observed that "much of the activity occurring during an encounter can be understood as an effort on everyone's part to get through the occasion and all the unanticipated and unintentional events that can cast participants in an undesirable light, without disrupting the relationships of the participants" (Goffman 1967, 41). For Goffman, the key to a successful conversation is not to manage how the other person is understanding what we're trying to say, but rather to manage our behaviors and responses such that both participants are able to create and maintain a positive self-image. In other words, to refer back to the discussion in chapter 4, the relational work (i.e., building positive relationships) of the conversation is primary, and provides the conditions that make the content work (i.e., communicating information) possible. Goffman proposes that in any given conversation, participants enter into a contract to protect one another's self-concept. If this is not done, it becomes impossible for the conversation to continue.

Goffman contends that we are rolling the dice on the outcome of each and every conversation. He has observed that we all work hard (although we might not have noticed, because this occurs naturally) within conversations to avert relational disaster and essentially to ensure that the encounter goes as smoothly as possible. His famous essay "On Face-Work" (Goffman 1967, 5–45) introduces and labels this idea as *face-work* and asserts that we are continually putting at risk our own self-image along with any previous goodwill we have established with the other person. Goffman says this about his definition of face-work: "By *face-work* I mean to designate the actions taken by a person to make whatever he is doing consistent with face" (Goffman 1967, 12; italics in original). Thus, we actively manage our identity, our "face," in every interaction through face-work that takes place through engaging in socially expected behavior, acting with respect, and being polite. In this way, we show respect toward others and expect that they will return this favor to us.

When face-work is not present, or politeness rituals are disrupted or ignored, Goffman calls these "face threats." These can happen innocently, or on purpose with the intent to insult or provoke (Brown and Levinson 1978, 14; Mon 2005). Goffman asserts that "face-work serves to counteract 'incidents'—that is, events whose effective implications threaten face" (Goffman 1967, 12). When someone's face has been threatened, face-work strategies (like avoidance or corrective process, such as an apology) must be offered to reestablish relational stability and to get back on firmer footing.

The work required to create and maintain face is often seen in interaction rituals, such as greeting rituals, closing rituals, and politeness rituals. Greetings and farewells are some of the most common interaction rituals we engage in on a daily basis, usually without paying much attention to them. We begin by saying "hello" and end with "good-bye." We remember and talk about when we last saw the other person or end with a statement about when we will meet again. Some variation of these rituals is done every time we meet someone and every time we take leave of them. These spoken greetings may be accompanied by a handshake for strangers and for formal or work-related occasions, or with a hug for close friends and family.

For example, think about the behaviors we see when a person approaches the reference desk. Before any interaction can take place, the face of each person must first be established by mutual acknowledgment of one another. It is natural for the librarian to look up and say "hi," or "how can I help you?" and perhaps make eye contact and smile. On Monday morning, when seeing our colleagues, we will say "good morning" or give another recognized greeting message, and perhaps ask about the weekend that just passed. On leaving for the day, we perform a leave-taking routine, often saying "bye" and a mention of when we will next meet such as "see you tomorrow!" Rituals are one type of face-work, because there are real consequences if these rituals are violated. For example, you may neglect to say good-bye to your colleague at the end of the day. To avoid any misinterpretation of this oversight (e.g., your work-mate thinking: "why is my colleague refusing to say goodbye to me?") you may feel compelled to mention it the next time you see her by saying something like, "Sorry I had to leave the meeting early yesterday. I did not get a chance to say good-bye, I had to run." Goffman calls such actions the *corrective process*. He contends that when a gaffe in face-work occurs, it must be repaired with an apology or explanation. Additionally, you may have noticed that in order for the corrective process to be resolved, the other person also has to acknowledge the apology (e.g., by saying "Oh, that's ok, I didn't think anything of it!"). If the other person does not acknowledge an apology, future conversations generally become strained, and the situation may deteriorate. In library environments where a large proportion of staff may be stable for many years, small slights can form the basis of yearlong resentments that may never be resolved. Goffman guides us in understanding these, using the lens of face-work (or lack thereof).

FACE IN REFERENCE ENCOUNTERS

The creation, maintenance, and protection of face is particularly pertinent to the participants in a reference encounter. Reference-related conversations generally take place between strangers, and, as such, much face-work must be done to establish the relative identities of the participants before the librarian can provide information or instruction to assist the user (Radford 1993, 1999, 2006a). A further complicating factor is that the library user may not know exactly what she is seeking, and may be unaware of, or intimidated by, the complexity of modern library systems (Radford and Radford 2005; Belkin, Oddy, and Brooks 1982). Also, with the ubiquitous presence of the Web (and search engines like Google and Bing) in our everyday lives, the ability of any information-literate individual to quickly and easily find high-quality information on any topic may be a given (Wellman and Haythornthwaite 2002). This expectation may instantly make the library user with a reference question feel unsophisticated and inadequate. Yet, despite all of the potential face threats inherent in any reference encounter, a person may still feel sufficiently motivated to approach a librarian and initiate a reference encounter. It is imperative, therefore, that the librarian be aware of and sensitive to these face-threat concerns.

Consider how important it is for a reference librarian at a public or academic library to be aware of her visible reactions to the subject matter about which a library user is seeking to find out more. The librarian must meet the inquiry with a friendly, professional attitude that implies to the user that her inquiry is being taken seriously. The librarian must do this in order to save the user's face, that is, the librarian treats the user as an intelligent person with a legitimate query. The librarian must also create and maintain a professional "face," that is, the librarian is a person who is knowledgeable and willing to assist. If the librarian were to react by giggling at an inquiry concerning an embarrassing medical question, for example, the user might leave the interaction and the library and never return because of shame or anger at not being given a professional response. Shame and guilt have been found to be present in reference encounters, especially those with younger users who have keen senses of fairness and may have fragile self-esteem in their adolescent years. Mary K. Chelton applied Goffman's framework and wrote about face threats and teenagers in her article "The 'Overdue Kid;' A Face-to-Face Library Service Encounter as Ritual Interaction" (Chelton 1997).

Goffman contends that "a promise to take ritual care of [his] face is built into the very structure of talk" (Goffman 1967, 40). So, we enter into a social contract to protect our own face and those of others whenever we are in a conversation. To fail to do so makes others think of us as rude, impolite, cold, or even manipulative. If an interaction is perceived as particularly positive, better face is established and we feel good about it. Perhaps we helped a client and they praised us enthusiastically, far beyond what we might expect. One of the authors can remember when she helped an older adult student at the reference desk at a university library years ago. He wrote her a short thank-you note on a piece of scrap paper and left it for her at the desk. This was unexpected, and she can still remember how good it made her feel to get this simple "thank-you." She saved this note and tacked it to her bulletin board for a very long time. It was memorable, because this small act of thankful-ness reinforced her sense of faith in herself as a "good reference librarian." She thus was able to establish a better face, through the student's overt and unusual written thank-you note.

When we feel that we are in positive face, we respond with confidence and assurance, and believe that we can hold our heads up high and openly present ourselves to others. We feel security and relief. Goffman says that we can "have face," "be in face," "maintain face," and also "give face" and "save face." When we are giving face, our actions make someone else look good. Perhaps someone made a social gaffe, and we use a sense of humor to minimize it. We both maintain and save face of others by covering their embarrassing moments in a nonjudgmental way. One special librarian reported that she often helped a physician with his research. However, he was not a good speller. One day while helping him, he asked for information on a topic that she could see he misspelled when entering it into an unforgiving search engine. He insisted his spelling was correct. A flash of inspiration occurred to her, and she said to him, "some people spell it this way" as she typed the correct spelling into the search box. Voilà—the sought-for information appeared and the doctor's pride was not hurt, because he was able to stay "in face" that is, that of being a medical expert. Thus, diplomacy skills in protecting and saving the face of others can come into play in establishing a good rapport with users and acting to prevent loss of face that contributes to unsuccessful interactions. Many times we do this naturally, without thinking about it. What is key in this example is that the librarian had a flash of inspi-ration and she acted on it. It may seem odd that she just did not simply say "you are spelling it wrong," but how would the doctor have taken this face threat when his mistake was pointed out? Embarrassment at being caught out of face would possibly have led to more awkward future interactions, or to him seeking out other librarians (or other libraries) in the future, using a tactic Goffman (1967) calls "avoidance" (see also Radford 2006b).

Another example comes from a large urban public library where a librarian noticed a man apparently having difficulty at the public photocopier. There were clear directions both on the machine and above the machine as to how to pay the ten cents per page cost and how to make the copies. The librarian watched in puzzlement as he became more agitated because he could not get the machine to work. She greeted him politely as he approached the service desk. In response to her greetings he replied loudly, "Here's my money, *you* make the copies!" He then slammed down a dollar bill on the desk. A bit shocked by his behavior, there were several sharp retorts that she could have said in reply, but again, this librarian had a flash of inspiration or intuition. She thought to herself, "I don't think he can read, that is why he is frustrated and angry." So, with this interpretation of his behavior in mind, she then said in a pleasant voice, "Would you like me to show you how, so you can do it yourself, this time and in the future?" The man looked very sheepish, lowered his eyes to his feet, and quietly said, "Yes, please." She showed him how to work the copier, and he thanked her for her help. The librarian had both protected his face by not giving him a sharp and shaming reply, and also her own face, by helping him to accomplish his task and showing him how to work the machine so he could do it next time. Additionally, she made a step towards building a positive professional interpersonal relationship with him. An unpleasant, even ugly, scene in the library that others would undoubtedly have witnessed was also avoided. What would have happened if the librarian had raised her voice, or quoted the rule book in response to his demand that she make the copies? How would this be interpreted by the man, or by onlookers?

Another example of face-work might be when you go out of your way to help a library user to find information, and then the user looks at his watch and hurries away, instead of thanking you for your time and effort. There may be many reasons for this abrupt departure (his class may be about to start, or perhaps he has an impending appointment), but the librarian may take this personally and feel slighted. From the client's point of view, it may be that the reference encounter with the librarian began with what he perceived as a sharp tone of voice from the librarian when she asked, "Have you looked in the online catalog?" From the librarian's point of view this is an innocent statement, but could be taken as a rebuke from the user's view, perhaps implying that he should not ask for help unless he has already begun his search in the appropriate library tool. Thus, the user's perceived failure to have first done some required (and maybe mysterious) task may result in feelings of shame and guilt, and a hesitation to approach the librarian next time (see also Radford 1999). The librarian may be completely unaware that some inadvertent nonverbal cue, whether it be a subtle change of pitch in the tone of voice, or perhaps a downward movement of the head as she peers over the top of her spectacles, has completely changed the user's response to her quite appropriate and innocent question. If users do not know, or are not confident, about where to start with research, any slight nonverbal cue may be taken as evidence of face threat. Research has found that questions along the lines of "have you already done x" (e.g., looked in the online catalog, searched a certain index, etc.) result in online chat users logging off rather than admitting that they had not "done x" (see DeAngelis 2010).

Active avoidance of future reference encounters may be the preferred course of action if a potential face threat is perceived. For example, a teenager asked for help finding a book at the adult services desk in an urban public library on a day when the young adult librarian was out. The reference librarian looked at the call number that the teen had provided, gave an annoyed look and pointed at the stacks, indicating that the book was "over there." The teen went in the direction of the pointing finger and searched the shelves, but ended up empty-handed because he was unable to find the book. When speaking up in a focus group interview, he said that he chose to leave the building, and to come back another day. His plan was to ask for help from another librarian (hopefully, he said, the young adult librarian who had helped him on several other occasions) rather than admit to this librarian that he failed to find the book on the shelf. He said that he found the librarian to be stern and condescending to him (Radford and Connaway 2007). This is an example of a classic avoidance strategy. If the librarian had been a bit friendlier, or had invited the teen to "come back if you don't find the book," the face threat and shaming experience would have been avoided. Teens are especially threat-avoidant, and less self-confident than many people understand, and because of this can be reluctant to admit when they do not know something. Thinking in terms of face-work and face threats can help us to better understand their reluctance to engage or self-disclose when they require help, and their avoidance behavior toward adults in positions of authority, such as librarians.

Another example was reported to one of the authors by a sixth-grade girl from the Bronx (Radford 2006b). She was at her local public library, doing her homework after school at a table with some friends when they became noisy and boisterous. The librarian came over and asked all of them to leave immediately. The girl said that although her friends were loud and were fooling around, she was doing her work. She said that the librarian was "accusing the innocent" and that, as a consequence of this unjust punishment, she would never return to that library. This perceived face threat and perceived unfair treatment resulted in an embarrassing and memorable incident that prompted this young girl to say that she would never come back, which is again a common avoidance strategy. It may be a surprise that this minor punishment would engender such a powerful emotional response in this young student that prompted her to never return; however, the authors have heard similar types of reactions, even from adults. In this case, what would have happened if the librarian had noticed which students were being noisy and given them a warning? Or another chance? Or if the librarian had assumed that the group was studying together and found them an individual group study room? There were likely many options that would have been less damaging to the individuals, as seen through the lens of face-work.

FACE-WORK IN A VIRTUAL REFERENCE ENCOUNTER

Reference service is a long-standing and integral part of nearly every library's mission, whether it takes the form of the traditional, in-person service desk approach, hybrid approaches which blend face-to-face (FtF) and online/virtual encounters, or other nontraditional approaches (such as reference encounters via social media, Skype, or librarians embedded in online courses or community groups). Of increasing importance, however, are the fully virtual experiences such as those conducted via live chat or instant messaging (IM) technology (see also Dempsey 2011; Lavoie 2008; Radford and Vine 2011; Smith and Pietraszewksi 2004; Zabel 2011). Web-based virtual reference services (VRS) that are offered by most academic and public libraries directly connect users to librarians via a chat window, where they can find help, instruction, and advice in real time. These chat services are generally available for extended hours; in the case of consortia arrangements, groups of libraries can collaborate to offer round-the-clock access to professionals every day of the year. Like instant message or chat via Facebook, the user and librarian communicate synchronously (or nearly so) with text-based messages, taken more-or-less in turns. The user first types in an initial query, and the librarian responds by engaging in a chat conversation to clarify the query and to provide assistance. Unlike FtF encounters that are mercurial and not generally recorded, one characteristic of chat reference is that a verbatim transcript is automatically produced by VRS systems that allow clients to review them later (e.g., for a list of URLs given for recommended web resources), and librarians to use for training and evaluation purposes.

In the VRS context, the interaction is formed in *the acts* of making (typing) verbal statements and in coordination with other statements to enable the participants to establish and maintain face. The participants must make choices concerning how these statements are presented and how they will respond to the statements of the other person. From the point of view of Goffman's framework, these choices, and their coordination by the participants, comprise the ritual behaviors that enable each participant to achieve both their information goals and also maintain their identity, self-worth, and face.

Live chat transcripts reveal that virtual interactions are remarkably similar to FtF reference encounters in that librarians and clients seek to establish a working partnership using elements that Goffman identified as important to positive interpersonal encounters. These elements include: greeting, closing, and politeness rituals, relationship building, and showing mutual respect and deference (Goffman 1967; Radford 2006a; Radford, Radford, Connaway, and DeAngelis 2011). However, on the negative side, text-based communication lacks many nonverbal cues (e.g., facial expressions and tone of voice) that help to build positive relationships, although we have created surrogates to express some of these cues, such as emoticons or emojis. Because there are so few nonverbal signals, both parties may sometimes experience increased feelings of frustration and impatience.

To serve as an example of this, the live chat transcript below was drawn from a large random sample collected from the QuestionPoint consortial live chat service (Radford and Connaway 2005–2008; Radford, Connaway, and Shah 2011–2014). Although most transcripts in these samples of chat sessions are positive or neutral in tone or nature, some clearly demonstrate face-work on the part of the librarian, the user, or both. This particular transcript is not typical, but was chosen as an example of the role of face-work in virtual reference interactions because of its unusually (and unfortunately) high number of instances of negative face threats. In fact, this is one of the most problematic examples of lack of face-work that the authors have seen among the thousands of chat transcripts they have read over a period of more than fifteen years of research.

This transcript centers on the question "When you drive forward in a bumper car at high speed and then you slam into the car in front of you, you find yourself thrown forward in your car. Which way is ur car accelerating?" The question appears to be a science homework question from a high school student who has sought the help of a librarian via chat. However, because all the users and librarians in the sample are required to remain anonymous for ethical reasons, we cannot confirm this from the transcript.

This transcript is reproduced verbatim, and thus misspellings, grammatical errors, and so forth have not been corrected (see the appendix for the complete transcript, which is 45 lines long, and runs a total of 17 minutes, 8 seconds. It may be helpful to read the full transcript before proceeding). It is useful to focus on this verbatim transcript because such things as spelling and punctuation are vital elements of the communication's context and thus have significance in the construction and maintenance of face. For example, both the librarian and the user can choose whether or not to send a message that contains typographical errors, a choice that may have an impact on the text's interpretation. Incorrect spelling may contribute to a perception of sloppiness, or the correction of a previously misspelled word may contribute to a perception of seriousness and attention to detail. Every aspect of the message's presentation has potential meaning, whether the sender of the message intends it or not. As mentioned, the interaction is 17 minutes, 8 seconds long, but there are no time stamps showing how much time has elapsed between replies. Below, the transcript is broken into small sections to help in the detailed discussion. In the transcript, "U" stands for User and "L" stands for Librarian. The interaction begins as follows:

Physics Transcript Lines 1–5

1	U	Physics
2	L	[Please hold for the next available librarian. If you would like a transcript of this session e-mailed to you, please type your full e-mail address now.]
3	L	[[Name]—A librarian has joined the session.]
4	U	when you drive forward in a bumper car at high speed and then you slam into the car in front of you, you find yourself thrown forward in your car. Which way is ur car accelerating?
5	L	thank you for holding I was working with another patron.

Let's take a close look at this initial part of the transcript, line-by-line, while keeping in mind that the greeting ritual is one of the important parts of Goffman's interaction ritual.

1   U   Physics

The user has been prompted by the system to enter a query in a box. The user has offered a broad category ("physics") rather than a particular question. Perhaps with the thought that a particular category of question will be directed toward a particular subject expert or librarian. Or perhaps the user is opening with a general category rather than a specific question because of the desire to ease into the encounter in a nonthreatening way; that is, by not initially revealing the detailed question.

2   L   [Please hold for the next available librarian. If you would like a transcript of this session e-mailed to you, please type your full e-mail address now.]

This is a scripted system greeting. It lets the user know that the question has been received and what to do to get a transcript of the session.

3   L   [[Name]—A librarian has joined the session.]

This is also scripted information. It lets the user know that the librarian is now present.

4   U   when you drive forward in a bumper car at high speed and then you slam into the car in front of you, you find yourself thrown forward in your car. Which way is ur car accelerating?

The user offers no "hello" or greeting ritual. Rather, the chat service is treated like an impersonal search engine, perhaps prompted to do so by the Google-like search box the system uses. In a FtF encounter, a simple greeting ritual like saying "hello" will often initiate the process of give and take that will establish a social bond between the participants. When there is no greeting, as in this interaction, there may be a negative effect on the ensuing conversation because a personal connection has not been established from the beginning. The user is also using the typing shortcut of "ur" for "your," which strongly suggests a younger user, perhaps a teenager. This informal use of a nonstandard abbreviation may suggest immaturity or a lack of seriousness to the librarian.

5   L   thank you for holding I was working with another patron.

The librarian has not acknowledged the user's question and there is no "hello" or other greeting. "Thank you for holding" is polite, but sounds impersonal, like a line from a telephone operator. The librarian does provide an explanation to the user for the wait time, which is a deferential and positive move that is common in normal face-work.

Physics Transcript Lines 6–11

6   L   Is this a homework question.
7   L   I'm not an expert on driving so I really can't answer that.
8   U   can u find a website or something
9   L   I'm not sure what you are asking.
10   U   when you drive forward in a bumper car at high speed and then you slam into the car in front of you, you find yourself thrown forward in your car. Which way is ur car accelerating?

11   U   ....

The greeting phase of the interaction has concluded, and now the librarian is performing a question negotiation, trying to gain clarification of the user's query. Again, let's take a closer look at how this critical beginning part of the encounter unfolds.

6   L   Is this a homework question.

This is a direct question to the user without any contextualizing or friendly tone. There is no "how are you?" or comment on the question (i.e., this question looks difficult or interesting or odd). This question can be superficially interpreted as a request for information. However, it can also easily be seen as a possible reprimand of the user for asking a homework question that by definition should be the work of the student, and should not be passed on to another person, such as the librarian. Interpreted this way, the inquiry "Is this a homework question" can be perceived as a face threat to the user, even if the librarian did not intend it this way. There are other ways that take a more neutral approach to finding out the background of the question, such as asking "Can you tell me more about this question?" (see Dervin and Dewdney 1986). The librarian has neglected to use the standard punctuation "?" at the end of the question, which might suggest that this is a hurried reply, or insufficient attention.

7   L   I'm not an expert on driving so I really can't answer that.

This statement implies that the user has asked the librarian personally for an answer to the question. Subject knowledge is not always present, but the librarian should nevertheless be able to provide a suggestion to help the student look for an appropriate site (which does occur later in the transcript when a URL from the Physics Classroom website is provided). The librarian's reply is not very helpful, and the librarian probably knows this. The statement is a disclaimer, a rebuff, and in actuality, a blatant refusal to help find an answer to the user's query. It is also a cue to the user that he or she may not be on the path to receiving an adequate answer from the librarian, who threatens the user's face with this statement of lack of expertise.

8   U   can u find a website or something.

The user is much more deferential here, recognizing the need to treat the librarian with more respect if he or she expects to receive the requested information. However, it also trivializes the librarian's expertise and sounds like a desperate plea. Here we also see another instance of the user adopting a typing short cut, in this case, "u" for "you," and using lower case instead of a capital letter at the beginning of sentences, although the librarian continues to use a very formal tone. The youth of the user is becoming more apparent, as does evidence of persistence. Despite the librarian's disclaimer of lack of knowledge, the user seems to be aware that some help could be obtained. Perhaps this user has had a positive encounter with the chat service in the past.

9   L   I'm not sure what you are asking.

Instead of offering the user reassurance that the librarian will help find an answer to the query, a disclaimer is again given. This statement acts as an obstacle to the user's quest to achieve a helpful answer. The librarian seems not to be working for mutual understanding, or engaging in relationship development, which is an appropriate response to a plea for help. This statement is also a face threat, because the implication is that the user's question is not clear.

10   U   when you drive forward in a bumper car at high speed and then you slam into the car in front of you, you find yourself thrown forward in your car. Which way is ur car accelerating?

The user seeks to overcome the obstacle produced by the librarian's second disclaimer by providing a restatement of the initial query. Because the wording is a verbatim copy of line 4, it is clear the user has cut and pasted this utterance, and has not attempted to rephrase the question in a manner that makes it more clear to both the librarian and the user. Again, perhaps experience with impersonal search engines, such as Google, may be prompting this type of reply.

11   U   . . . .

Although this transcript does not have time stamps to show how much time passes between the exchanges of the librarian and user, it is clear from the ellipses and "hello?" in lines 11 and 12 that the user is waiting for a response from the librarian. The absence of any kind of response is itself a powerful message that communicates a negative attitude toward the user. Providing face-work in the form of "word-contact," such as a reassurance that "I'm still working," would be an appropriate textual equivalent of nodding or eye contact in FtF encounters.

Physics Transcript Lines 12–15

```
12    U   hello?
13    L   Is this a homework a homework assignment. what subject is it.
14    L   I really don't understand how I can answer that for you.
15    U   can i hav another librarian.
12    U   hello?
```

The user again seeks to discover if the librarian is still connected because there have been no confirming messages sent.

```
13    L   Is this a homework a homework assignment. what subject is it.
```

The librarian does not explain the delay in reply, offer an apology for being away from the interaction, or explain that perhaps a search has taken time to look for information to answer the user's question. Perhaps the service is busy, and the librarian has been helping other users in the queue. The librarian does not offer reassurance that she will pursue the query, but instead repeats the face-threatening question regarding the homework assignment. This line indicates that perhaps the librarian is not fully engaged, and communicates a message of distrustfulness and inattention. Asking what subject the question is from also shows that the librarian is not paying enough attention--in line 1 the user identifies the subject as "physics."

```
14    L   I really don't understand how I can answer that for you.
```

The librarian comes back a third time with a disclaimer (as in lines 7 and 9), which is an attempt to push the user away again. This response sends a disconfirming message by indicating that the user's attempt to use VRS to find an answer may be misguided. In essence, such a remark to the user acts as a type of rejection of the question and also of the person. The face threat is unmistakable. The librarian wants the user to go away, an example of a negative closure strategy identified by Ross and Dewdney (1998). In essence, the librarian is trying to end the encounter without answering the user's question.

```
15    U   can i hav another librarian
```

This is a disconfirming comment by the user, who responds to the librarian's messages of rejection with a similar rejection. In lines 14–15, a breech in politeness is apparent, and some form of repair should have been attempted by the user, perhaps along the lines of a face-saving apology. A process of face-repair would normally be engaged when a communication interaction is recognized as potentially threatening one's own face or the face of the other. The user tries an avoidance strategy in line 15 by acknowledging the librarian's unwillingness or inability to help and requesting to have "another librarian." This request can be considered a direct face threat to the librarian. Because neither participant engages in a corrective process (i.e., an apology or explanation), this lack of face-work contributes to the further deterioration of the interaction. The user continues to use shortcuts, lower case, and abbreviations and to be less formal than the librarian.

Physics Transcript Lines 16–21

16   L   The information you gave you me does not help me find any resources to help you.

17   L   What do you mean by which way is your car accerlaerating. Are you sure thats what your assignment asks.

18   U   Yes

19   L   What subject is this question from?

20   C   Physics

21   L   Okay just one moment.

16   L   The information you gave you me does not help me find any resources to help you.

Usually librarians engage in query clarification to elicit additional information from users so that the query can be better understood and addressed. Often librarians formulate open-ended or neutral questions such as, "Can you tell me more about what you need?" and the user can then respond to inform the search process (see Ross, Nilsen, and Radford 2009; Dervin and Dewdney 1986). Rather than ask clarifying questions, or acknowledge the user's request for another librarian, the librarian's disclaimer mirrors the user's behavior with a face threat. The librarian implies again that it is the user's fault that the interaction is failing.

17   L   What do you mean by which way is your car accerlaerating. Are you sure thats what your assignment asks.

The librarian continues with more questions about the assignment, but asks what the assignment is, rather than what the user wants to know. The user has yet to disclose whether this is a homework assignment, and as yet nothing definite is known about the user's age or educational status. The librarian's implication that the user does not understand the assignment is condescending and represents another threat to the user's face. The librarian is also making spelling mistakes ("accerlaerating" and leaving the apostrophe out of "that's"), which may indicate a hurried rush or insufficient attention.

18   U   Yes

Although the user replies "yes" it is unclear if the reply addresses the librarian's question in line 13 or about the assignment in line 17. This asynchronous nature of live chat further complicates the communication process.

19   L   What subject is this question from?

The librarian demonstrates a lack of attention to the interaction by asking for the subject of the question again (as in line 13), because this information was present in line 1.

20   C   Physics

The user answers the question without demonstrating impatience, which is polite, especially given the back and forth about this question, and that line 1 had already provided the answer.

21   L   Okay just one moment.

After the user provides the subject again, the librarian indicates for the first time that some time is needed and that help will be provided to the user. This is followed by the librarian pushing a series of web pages from the Physics Classroom. The pages are sent quickly, without waiting for the user to have a chance to look at them. These would open in a rapid string, one after another, in the user's browser.

Physics Transcript Lines 22–32

22   L   [Web Page sent]
23   L   This is one site that may help.
24–25 L   [Pages sent]
26   L   this is another site that youmay try forhelp.

27   L   When we disconnect youwill have these links in a transcript.
28   L   [Page sent]
29   L   This site looks to be very helpful.
30–32 L   [Pages sent]
22   L   [Web Page sent]

It is unusual that it has taken twenty-two lines before any web page is sent to the user. Generally something is sent within the first ten or so lines, after the librarian understands the question and begins to search for online resources.

23   L   This is one site that may help.

The librarian's use of the phrase "may help" communicates that whether the website is actually useful is unknown, and potentially that the librarian does not care, a face threat to the user.

24–25 L   [Pages sent]

The librarian continues to push pages to the user, but does not seek any feedback as to whether these pages were actually useful.

26   L   this is another site that youmay try forhelp.

The librarian's tentative "may try" suggests that its usefulness is in question. Again, some inattention to proper spacing may indicate rushing. Is the librarian helping more than one user at once? If so, informing the user would have been a face-work strategy to explain some of the inattention revealed by repeated questions.

27   L   When we disconnect youwill have these links in a transcript.

The librarian provides helpful information here, but the user does not respond until line 33, and then gives a negative response.

28   L   [Page sent]
29   L   This site looks to be very helpful.

In Line 29 the librarian gives a personal evaluation of the site pushed in line 28, but again fails to ask the user for any feedback, showing a lack of deference.

The librarian seems to be paying more attention here, but it is perhaps too late to save this encounter.

30–32　L　[Pages sent]

Physics Transcript Lines 33–38

33	U	this isn't helpful
34	L	Well I really don't have any other resources that can assit you.
35	L	[Page sent]
36	L	I cannot answer the question for you, I don't have the physics knowledge.
37	L	Maybe you will need to ask your instructor for a clear understanding.
38	L	[Page sent]
33	U	this isn't helpful

The user's statement is again disconfirming to the librarian and represents another face threat. At this point in the interaction, it could be concluded that the librarian has experienced a loss of face, because the librarian's primary responsibility in the interaction is to provide the user with information to answer the query. In this sense, the librarian has failed. But it is not only the information pushed that is not helpful. The user could also be saying that the librarian's behavior of pushing a series of several websites, without asking for feedback or clarification, is also unhelpful.

34　　L　Well I really don't have any other resources that can assit you.

The librarian responds with another disclaimer, which combined with other disclaimers constitute failure to make an appropriate referral for the user. This ultimately means that the user may leave the session empty-handed. However, the librarian does send another page, but again fails to tell the user what the page is or how it might be useful in addressing the query.

35　　L　[Page sent]

The librarian once more returns to sending a web page to the user despite the fact that the user has just stated that the web pages are not helpful.

36　　L　I cannot answer the question for you, I don't have the physics knowledge.

The librarian realizes that the appropriate information to address the user's query cannot be found, and offers a reason in an attempt to repair face: that is, the librarian does not have the needed physics knowledge. It also signals that the librarian will stop working on the question. This is also similar to the disclaimer, in line 7, that the librarian has no driving expertise. This late in the transcript, the damage is done; there is seemingly no redemption that could repair it to restore a climate of mutual respect.

37   L   Maybe you will need to ask your instructor for a clear understanding.

The user has never offered the information that this query is motivated by a homework assignment, so the librarian's referral here is another face threat and a very late attempt at a referral. This can be seen as another example of "negative closure" (Ross and Dewdney 1998), or trying to end the encounter (in this case with sending the user to the instructor) without answering the user's question.

38   L   [Page sent]

The librarian persists in sending more web pages to the user, despite the absence of any positive feedback that these are helpful.

Physics Transcript Lines 39–45

39   U   do u kno ne1 who does
40   L   [Page sent]
41   L   Sorry I do not.
42   U   ok
43   L   I have a few patron that I ned to assist.
44   U   ok bye
45   L   [Thank you for using [VRS]! If you have any further questions, please contact us again.]
39   U   do u kno ne1 who does

The user responds by asking if the librarian knows anyone (ne1) with a working knowledge of physics. The user has ignored the pages the librarian sent and does not say whether they are useful. The user is ready to end the interaction and talk to someone else who is more knowledgeable about the query's subject matter. In essence, the user knows that a referral is possible, and is again attempting to use the face-work strategy of avoidance. This particular line sounds like a sad plea for help from the user, who is realizing with growing certainty that assistance is not coming from this librarian. The use of "ne1" for "anyone" is an ongoing reminder of the difference in age and formality level between the user and the librarian. It is interesting that despite the face threats and inattention in this interaction the user is still not ready to give up, but is continuing to seek some kind of assistance from the librarian.

40   L   [Page sent]

The librarian continues to send pages, even though the user has indicated that they are not helpful, both in an explicit statement to that effect and by ignoring all the subsequent websites previously pushed by the librarian. One of the ironic aspects of this transcript is that several of the pages sent from the Physics Classroom would have been helpful to the student in answering the question. There would not be a direct answer, but rather, information about Newton's laws of motion, an understanding of which is necessary to answer the question about bodies in motion (the bumper cars).

41   L   Sorry I do not.

This statement could be read literally, that is, the librarian does not know someone with a knowledge of physics, or it could he read as saying that she does not want to deal with this question, which is an affront to the user's face. Although this may look like an apology because of the use of the word "sorry," it does not meet Goffman's (1967) criteria of appearing sincere, given the context and content of the preceding forty lines. If the librarian was sincerely sorry, there were options for referral that could have been shared. The user has a sense of this, as evidenced by line 39, "do u kno ne1 who does."

42   U   ok

The user acknowledges the librarian's statement, and is probably aware that no further useful information, either about the query or how to go about answering the query, is going to be forthcoming from this interaction. The user is giving up.

43   L   I have a few patron that I ned to assist.

The librarian acknowledges that the interaction is over, but does not apologize for failing to provide the information. The librarian does not wish the user well in seeking an answer. Rather, the librarian demeans the status of the user by stating that there are other users to help, presumably with queries that are more important, or better stated, or are not merely homework questions. Another misspelling may indicate a rushed departure.

44   U   ok bye

The user offers a ritual closing statement, which is a face-work move, as if attempting a positive (if unsuccessful) conclusion.

45   L   [Thank you for using [VRS]! If you have any further questions, please contact us again.]

The librarian fails to conclude the interaction with a personalized closing statement, choosing to push a prepared script, once more demeaning the user's status. The scripted invitation to contact the service again, despite the failed encounter, can be interpreted as insincere and robotic, even though it may have been pushed automatically by the system rather than by the librarian. The user is further threatened here by the librarian's insincere invitation to return, which undoubtedly will be recognized as a script.

FACE-WORK AND FACE THREAT IN THE PHYSICS/ BUMPER CAR TRANSCRIPT

The Physics/Bumper Car transcript, though uncomfortable to read, is an important one, because it reveals tension that occurs in online interactions, especially if face-work is inappropriate and no corrective processes are put in place when face threats loom. In this sequence of typed chat messages, a struggle unfolds between the librarian and user, as each attempts to push forward to reach their respective goals. The user wants help answering a question, and the librarian's goal is to provide reference service to assist the user by answering the question or providing instruction (Radford 1999, 2006a). However, Goffman (1967) also tells us that in addition, both participants need to get through this encounter with self-esteem and face intact. None of these goals are accomplished in this session, with potentially damaging interpersonal effects.

The face threat begins early in the transcript, right after an initial and positive deference move in line 5, when the librarian thanks the user for holding, explaining that he or she was helping another person. This positivity, however, is immediately negated in line 6, where a lack of deference is shown in the flat inquiry "is this a homework question." Indeed, if this is not a homework question, it would be a great surprise to anyone who has taken a physics class (or similar science, or even a math class) in the United States. It is a classic example of a question that would be difficult to imagine as not being a homework question. Rather, it is easily and unmistakably recognizable as a quintessential homework question. Although the librarian's question about its origin may be interpreted as an innocent query to gather information about the nature of the physics question, it actually serves to construct a relational barrier that pushes back at the user. This barrier is formed because the question calls attention to the core idea of homework, which requires that students do their own work. The librarian's repeated questions (again in line 13) about the nature of the question, and the subject matter (also asked about in line 19), suggests that it may not be appropriate to ask for reference help for school-related questions. The strong implication here is that homework questions are not valid questions for VRS, and that the user is behaving inappropriately by asking one.

Another aspect of this encounter that may have led to the multiple questions about homework, as well as the librarian attempting a referral in line 37 to "ask your instructor," is that the asker is definitely presenting herself as a young person, most likely in high school, when physics is typically taught as part of the standard science curriculum. Research that compared librarian behavior toward adolescents (or young adults in college) to that with older adults found that older adults are generally treated with more respect and deference (see Connaway and Radford 2010; Connaway, Radford, Dickey, Williams, and Confer 2008; and Radford and Connaway 2007).

The librarian's assertion to "not be an expert on driving," (line 7) or in physics (line 36) poses additional barriers. Reference librarians are information specialists, educated in the procedures of identifying and locating information. The librarian's unwillingness to locate information on physics (or to make a referral, even when directly asked by the user in lines 15 and 39) shows a lack of commitment to providing service. Requests for information are considered face-threatening acts because they require a response from the librarian, who must be active to preserve his or her own face (as an expert), while simultaneously attending to the positive face of the user. Other requests made by the librarian to this young user are also face-threatening acts, such as requesting information about what this user did to understand the question and to investigate the subject matter of the question before logging on to the chat service (DeAngelis 2010).

The user is remarkably persistent, given the series of face threats that occur in this transcript. Instead of addressing the personal information in the form of disclaimers by the librarian (e.g., the lack of physics or driving knowledge), the user pushes back to request a bare minimum of assistance, "a website or something." The user could have understood the librarian's disclosure of a lack of expertise to imply that he or she either did not care to answer the question, or as a statement of truth. Either way, the user could have just dropped the question and logged off at any time. However, the user chooses to continue the conversation, although more negative face-work is in store when the librarian says: "I'm not sure what you are asking" (line 9). This flat statement of uncertainty by the librarian about the user's request, without any softening explanation, gives further evidence of a lack of face-work.

The negative face-work continues on the part of both participants, and perhaps reaches a peak in line 15, when the user asks, "can I hav another librarian." This request announces to the librarian that the user has reached the conclusion that the librarian is incapable of finding an answer to the query and another librarian's help should be sought. This request is an outright rejection, and asserts the incompetence or unwillingness of the librarian to lend aid. As a retort, in line 16 the librarian blames the user for providing insufficient information that "does not help me find any resources." After taking jabs at one another, the participants eventually settle into a more typical relationship. At line 19, the librarian types "Okay just one minute," generally accepted in chat as a request for the user to hold on while the librarian searches for resources.

This is the first point in the transcript (coming at last halfway through the 17-minute session) that the librarian demonstrates willingness to help the user by beginning the search process. One explanation for this delay in beginning a search may be that the librarian had several chat windows open (or even may have been staffing a physical service desk) and may have been distracted. However, if this is the case, some apology or explanation when leaving for long periods of time, or when asking again about the topic of the question, would have been in order as a show of respect for the user. A corrective process through explanation or apology would have helped to rescue this session, but did not occur.

Help was provided to the user only in the form of "drive by reference" (Laura Kortz, personal communication), in which the librarian sends URLs for one web page after another (see lines 22, 24, 28, 30, 35, and 38) in rapid succession. This course of action places a rush of informational web pages between librarian and user. The librarian appears unwilling to take the user through the websites one at a time to determine if they meet the user's need, or even to get feedback before sending additional sites. By sending a stream of web pages, the librarian is limiting interaction, which demonstrates another relational barrier and one more form of face threat. The user interjects in line 33 that the websites are not "helpful." Again, this reveals that the user is dissatisfied with the librarian's help, which is a type of insult and which sends a disconfirming message to the librarian. Another signal of dissatisfaction is seen in the user's second request to get help from another person. In line 39, the user asks if the librarian knows "ne1 [anyone] who does" [have the needed physics knowledge]. This overt disapproval is another intense form of face threat.

In chat encounters, librarians usually have the option to refer the user to other information professionals for assistance, or to offer to have themselves, or have another librarian get back to the user with information, usually via e-mail. Instead of making a referral, the librarian responds to the user's second request for someone else with an apology and the flat reply, "I do not." This unwillingness to provide a referral again makes it clear that the librarian does not want to help, and also actively blocks the user's progress toward resolution. In the end, the librarian has left the user with an unresolved and relationally damaging conclusion. The librarian sends a message in line 43 that he or she must leave to help another, perhaps more worthy, user. The user accepts defeat in line 44 and completes the closing ritual by saying "ok bye." Ironically, as noted above, some of the websites that were sent in rapid succession could have proven useful, had the librarian pointed out the particular parts that referred to Newton's laws, which were, of course, at the heart of this bumper car question.

This transcript offers insight into how various forms of negative face-work, active face threats, and other disconfirming messages block the interaction's success. Goffman's concept of face-work provides a constructive framework to analyze and make sense of this interaction. When face-work is executed wisely, participants feel good about their interactions, feel good about themselves, and feel good about the other person, because the messages support their presentation of self. Positive face-work enhances positive impression management and interpersonal relationship development. When confronted with conflict in the form of negative face-work, face threats, and outright attacks, those involved leave an encounter without confirmation of self. In general terms, the success of any service interaction (whether FtF or in computer-mediated VRS contexts) depends to a large extent on the participant's ability to manage face-work to show support for his or her own face and for the face of the other.

The Physics/Bumper Car transcript provides an example of both failure to deliver appropriate information and failure to show support for one another's face. Although this transcript is not at all representative of chat reference encounters in general, it provides a genuine account of how face threats and other forms of negative face-work act as barriers to providing an answer or instruction, and demonstrates the types of collisions that occur and the outcomes of a process largely free of face-work. It also serves as an excellent example of an unsuccessful encounter that illustrates a relational model of reference encounters, which will be presented in chapter 6.

REFERENCES

Belkin, Nicholas, Robert N. Oddy, and Helen M. Brooks. 1982. "ASK for Information Retrieval: Part 1: Background and Theory." *Journal of Documentation* 38 (2): 61–71.

Brown, Penelope, and Stephen Levinson. 1987. *Politeness: Some Universals in Language Usage.* Cambridge, UK: Cambridge University Press.

Chelton, Mary K. 1997. "The 'Overdue Kid': A Face-to-Face Library Service Encounter as Ritual Interaction." *Library and Information Science Research* 9 (4): 387 – 99.

Connaway, Lynn S., and Marie L. Radford. 2010. "Virtual Reference Service Quality: Critical Components for Adults and the Net-Generation." *Libri* 60 (2): 165–80.

Connaway, Lynn. S., Marie. L. Radford, Timothy J. Dickey, Jocelyn D. Williams, and Patrick C. Confer. 2008. "Sense-Making and Synchronicity: Information-Seeking Behaviors of Millennials and Baby Boomers." *Libri* 58: 123–35.

DeAngelis, Jocelyn A. 2010. "Friction in Computer-Mediated Communication: An Unobtrusive Analysis of Face Threats Between Librarians and Users in the Virtual Reference Context." PhD diss., Rutgers, The State University of New Jersey.

Dempsey, Megan. 2011. "Blending the Trends: A Holistic Approach to Reference Services." *Public Services Quarterly* 7 (1–2): 3–17.

Dervin, Brenda, and Patricia Dewdney. 1986. "Neutral Questioning: A New Approach to the Reference Interview." *RQ,* 25 (4): 506–13.

Goffman, Erving. 1959. *The Presentation of Self in Everyday Life.* Garden City, New York: Doubleday Anchor.

———. 1964. "The Neglected Situation." *American Anthropologist* 66: 133–36.

———. 1967. *Interaction Ritual: Essays on Face-to-Face Behavior.* Garden City, New York: Doubleday.

Lavoie, Lisa. 2008. "Roving Librarians: Taking It to the Streets." *Urban Library Journal* 15 (1): 78–82.

Manusov, Valerie, and Miles L. Patterson. 2006. *The Sage Handbook of Nonverbal Communication.* Thousand Oaks, CA: Sage.

Mon, Lorri. 2005. "Face Threat." In *Theories of Information Behavior,* edited by Karen E. Fisher, Sanda Erdelez, and Lynne McKechnie, 149–52. Medford, NJ: ASIST.

Radford, Gary P., and Marie L. Radford. 2005. "Structuralism, Post-Structuralism, and the Library: De Saussure and Foucault." *Journal of Documentation* 51 (1): 60–78.

Radford, Marie L. 1993. "Relational Aspects of Reference Interactions: A Qualitative Investigation of the Perceptions of Users and Librarians in the Academic Library." PhD diss., Rutgers, The State University of New Jersey.

———. 1999. *The Reference Encounter: Interpersonal Communication in the Academic Library.* Chicago: Association of College and Research Libraries.

———. 2006a. "Encountering Virtual Users: A Qualitative Investigation of Interpersonal Communication in Chat Reference." *Journal of the American Society for Information Science and Technology* 57 (8): 1046–59.

———. 2006b. "The Critical Incident Technique and the Qualitative Evaluation of the Connecting Libraries and Schools Project." *Library Trends* 54 (1): 46–64.

Radford, Marie L., and Lynn S. Connaway. 2005–2008. *Seeking Synchronicity: Evaluating Virtual Reference Services from User, Non-User, and Librarian Perspectives.* Dublin, OH: OCLC Research. www.oclc.org/research/themes/user-studies/synchronicity.html.

———. 2007. "'Screenagers' and Live Chat Reference: Living Up to the Promise." *Scan* 26 (1): 31–39.

Radford, Marie L., Lynn S. Connaway, and Chirag Shah. 2011–2014. *Cyber Synergy: Seeking Sustainability through Collaboration between Virtual Reference and Social Q&A Sites.* OCLC Research. www.oclc.org/research/activities/synergy/default.htm.

Radford, Marie L., Gary P. Radford, Lynn S. Connaway, and Jocelyn A. DeAngelis. 2011. "On Virtual Face-Work: An Ethnography of Communication Approach to a Live Chat Reference Interaction." *The Library Quarterly* 81 (4): 431–53.

Radford, Marie L., and Scott Vine. 2011. "An Exploration of the Hybrid Service Model: Keeping What Works." In *Reference Reborn: Breathing New Life into Public Services Librarianship,* edited by Diane Zabel, 79–89. Denver, CO: Libraries Unlimited.

Ross, Catherine S., and Patricia Dewdney. (1998). "Negative Closure: Strategies and Counter-Strategies in the Reference Transaction." *Reference and User Services Quarterly* 38 (2): 151–63.

Ross, Catherine S., Kirsti Nilsen, and Marie L. Radford. 2009. *Conducting the Reference Interview,* 2nd ed., New York: Neal-Schuman.

Smith, Michael. M., and Barbara A. Pietraszewski. 2004. "Enabling the Roving Reference Librarian: Wireless Access with Tablet PCs." *Reference Services Review* 32 (3): 249–55.

Wellman, Barry, and Caroline Haythornthwaite. 2002. "The Internet in Everyday Life: An Introduction." In *The Internet in Everyday Life,* edited by Barry Wellman and Caroline Haythornthwaite, 3–41. Malden, MA: Blackwell.

Zabel, Diane. 2011. *Reference Reborn: Breathing New Life into Public Services Librarianship,* 79–89. Denver, CO: Libraries Unlimited.

Zornoza, Ana, Pilar Ripoll, and José M. Peiró. 2002. "Conflict Management in Groups that Work in Two Different Communication Contexts: Face-to-Face and Computer-Mediated Communication." *Small Group Communication* 33 (5): 481–508.

A Content/Relational Model of Success in Reference Encounters

There are many types of encounters that take place in and around libraries (both physical and virtual), and previous chapters have explored some of these, including colleague-to-colleague, manager-to-subordinate, and service-desk scenarios. One specialized and quite complex type of interaction occurs in the context of the reference encounter, as previously overviewed in our Physics/Bumper Car transcript example of live chat reference in chapter 5. These goal-oriented conversations between a librarian and a library user happen within a specific type of situation that we are all familiar with, whether at a physical or virtual library reference desk, or via phone. These generally include talk that centers on a reference query. We believe that the nature of reference encounters brings into sharp focus the dual aspects of content (information) and relational (interpersonal) dimensions, and the need for wise use of face-work and avoidance of face threats, in ways far more profound than everyday conversations.

When a library user's attempts to find information on his or her own fail, or if they do not know where to start, they may choose to approach a librarian at a brick or click reference desk. When they do, the librarian becomes the human mediator between the library's knowledge base and complex systems and the person's information need. The interaction takes on all the relational dimensions of any conversation, professional or otherwise. However, the reference encounter also takes on a particular importance. When successful, it can become the point at which the complexities of the library are gently explained, fears are calmed, and information made accessible. Or, on the other hand, if help is given in a grudging, hurried, or condescending manner, the encounter can become the critical point where the library appears even more inaccessible and library users can be left feeling confused, frustrated, or even humiliated.

In this chapter we present an original model of the reference encounter, firmly based on the principles of the relational view of interpersonal communication and related theories that have been introduced in chapters 1 through 5. These include ideas from Aristotle; John Locke; Ruesch and Bateson; Watzlawick, Beavin Bavelas, and Jackson; and Goffman. The relational view of interpersonal communication offers a theoretically rich account of library interactions. It is possible that you may think that a model of interpersonal communication based on relational principles may be somewhat of a contradiction. After all, one objective of a theoretical model is to enable individuals to predict and possibly control related phenomena. However, as has been shown previously, interpersonal communication encounters are intrinsically unpredictable and completely contingent upon unique situational contexts, and the previous (if any) relationship between the participants. This is the case even under very controlled conditions. For example, facilitators in communication skills workshops often attempt to demonstrate the relevance and impact of interpersonal encounters in professional contexts through the use of role-playing exercises. One person may play the role of manager, another plays the role of an employee, and a typical conversation is played out. But even here, no two role-played conversations are ever the same. These, too, are dependent upon the situation in which they occur (that is, a training workshop in the presence of a facilitator and possibly an audience of other participants who may be coworkers or supervisors/supervisees). The background, experiences, enthusiasm, or shyness of the participants, their prior relationship, how they are feeling that day, and so on, will also have a bearing on the communication behaviors that are exhibited. However, it is still tempting to compare the performance in the exercise against what a so-called idealized skilled communicator would do. It is very easy to "check off the boxes" and say you should have done this, this, and this, but not this, this, or that.

This approach fails to recognize the uniqueness of each interaction, the intricacies of the previous relationships of those involved, and how the conversation can develop in unexpected ways. This unpredictability is not an anomaly of conversation. This is what conversations are, including those that take place in library contexts. Therefore, one cannot manage reference encounters in a strictly strategic sense. Rather, one must employ the principles of practical wisdom to best navigate the currents of any ongoing conversation. The model does not claim to predict communication behavior, nor prescribe what the best communication behavior should be in every communication situation. Instead, the model seeks to classify the sources of uncertainty and contingency rather than predict and control them. Then the professional will be in the best position to identify what is going on, and act according to the practical wisdom appropriate for that unique situation. The model explicitly recognizes and incorporates these principles in a way that can inform participants how and why a reference encounter may be deemed to be successful or unsuccessful.

THE MODEL

The Content/Relational Model of Success in Reference Encounters shown in figure 6.1 is based on copious research gathered over several decades that focused on library service interactions in face-to-face (FtF) and online environments.[1] This innovative model is intended to be a tool to help us understand (and perhaps improve) interpersonal encounters in the professional context.

The model highlights the critical importance of a combination of positive content and relational dimensions of communication and how these affect perceptions of success (or lack thereof) in reference encounters. The research that underpins this model is based largely on evidence from three groups: librarians, library users (including virtual reference service [VRS] users), and VRS nonusers. A chorus of their voices gave testimony about satisfaction and success (or lack thereof) in numerous focus groups, observations, online surveys, face-to-face or phone interviews, and live chat VRS transcripts (see Radford 1993; 1999; Radford and Connaway 2005–2008; Radford, Connaway, and Shah 2011–2014).

The Encounter Context

The model consists of an outer ring that contains the Encounter Context, which surrounds and affects reference outcomes. The interior of the model represents in graphic form the relative success of a reference encounter along two axes consisting of the dimensions of content (did the user receive/librarian provide the appropriate content?) and the relational (did the user and the librarian feel comfortable within the interaction?) At the bottom of the model are boxes that list the important factors for the content dimensions and the relational dimensions, as identified by extensive research.

FIGURE 6.1

Content/Relational Model of Success in Reference Encounters

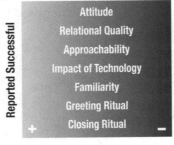

Created by Marie L. Radford and Lynn Silipigni Connaway. © 2015 Marie L. Radford and OCLC

Let's take a closer look at the model. The first part is its surrounding circle which recognizes the overarching importance of the multitude of factors that make up the reference encounter's context. As noted above, no encounter takes place in a vacuum. As in all conversations, the context will always have an intrinsic part to play before a single word has been uttered and will, indeed, profoundly impact the words that will be uttered (or typed, in the case of virtual encounters).

Mode

The model acknowledges that there is a growing range of communication modes (and combinations of them) that users and librarians can select for engaging in reference encounters. Such modes include FtF, phone, e-mail, VRS (live chat) or instant message (IM) encounters, as well as those accessed through social media and on mobile devices. Also, modes can vary and be combined in various ways within encounters. Sometimes a reference query starts out as an e-mail or a chat, but then ends up as a phone call or FtF visit.

Participant Characteristics

The model recognizes that each participant is an individual who has a unique range of personal characteristics including age, gender, cultural background, level of education, language skills, language facility, information literacy, technological skills, subject knowledge, communication skills, institutional affiliation, a librarian's previous experience and reference service philosophy, a user's past experience with libraries and librarians, and more.

Situation

Each reference encounter is a unique situation in itself. Reference queries are related to a complex array of situations including: professional, academic, personal, or other (see Savolainen 2005). They may originate from the users of public, academic, special, consortial, or other types of libraries, library websites, or via phones or mobile apps. There may be a time constraint for one or both of the participants (or group of participants). There may be constraints on the participants' ability to access needed resources, such as physical distance, disabilities, language proficiency, limited or no connectivity to online resources, or lack of affiliation to a university/college/public library or consortium.

What Is a Reference Encounter?

We deliberately refer to the interaction between the user and the librarian, whether FtF, via phone, or online, as an *encounter*. This term is intentionally chosen, as opposed to a term like "interaction" or "conversation," and has important implications for how this situation is understood. The reference interaction is an example of a "social situation," using Goffman's (1964) definition (given in chapter 5) and involves "mutual monitoring." Ruesch and Bateson also identify awareness and mutual monitoring as perhaps the single most important aspect of interpersonal communication, even before a single word has been spoken. They write:

> A social situation is established as soon as an exchange of communication takes place; and such an exchange begins with the moment in which the actions of the other individuals are perceived as responses—that is, as evoked by the sender's message and therefore as comments upon that message, giving the sender an opportunity of judging what the message meant to the receiver. (Ruesch and Bateson [1951] 1968)

Such *communication about communication* must be present if any subsequent exchange of messages is to take place. This *perception of the perception* is "the sign that a silent agreement has been reached by the participants, to the effect that mutual agreement is to be expected" and that "the mutual recognition of having entered into each other's field of perception equals the establishment of a system of communication" (Ruesch and Bateson [1951] 1968, 23–24). When we are engaged in our FtF conversations, we can certainly perceive the nonverbal accompaniments of a verbal message and we attempt, for better or worse, to make sense of the verbal message within the context of those behaviors. People might accompany their messages with a smile, a frown, or an eyebrow raise, or by looking at the floor when they speak. The other person might also be aware of the potential impact these behaviors might have on the reception and perception of their utterances. We have our nonverbal acts, and we have our awareness that others are aware of those acts, and know that these acts may cause others to modify their perceptions of our behaviors. Goffman (1967) calls this constant attention and response to the actions of the other "embodied perception." It is not just that one person acts and then the other person responds in some linear fashion. The other person is also *aware* of our looking and listening, and responds accordingly. Therefore, even our act of perception has message value. Each message is also a response, and that response is also a message, simultaneously. When I speak to you, you communicate to me that you are listening. Your listening is *both* an act of perception *and* a message to me. It tells me that "you are listening." This may seem like a very trivial statement, but it has significant implications for the manner in which reference encounters play out in the professional workplace.

Once people have entered into communication, it is left to them to identify the social situation. They need to answer the question: What are we doing here? Each person may have his/her own views regarding the nature of the situation. Much confusion can result when the participants disagree as to what a situation is about. For example, if a student asks a ready reference question, should the librarian give the answer, or provide instruction in how to find the answer? If the student expects the answer and gets instruction, he or she may be disappointed, and perhaps frustrated. If the librarian expects that the student wants instruction, there will be disappointment and frustration when the student demands the answer. The labeling of the situation, as well as the goals, is at odds here. The goal of the student is to get the answer, of the librarian it is to give instruction (Radford 1993, 1999). Conflict and perceptions of lack of success can result. In this example, the librarian assumed the role of "teacher." Through communication with others, roles are *mutually* assigned. The term "role" refers to nothing but the code that is used to interpret the flow of messages. Awareness of a person's role in a social situation enables others to gauge the meaning of her statements and actions.

Goffman's notion of the *encounter* is derived from this process of mutual attention and mutual monitoring. Goffman defines the encounter as: "Two or more people in a social situation who jointly ratify one another as authorized co-sustainers of a single focus of visual and cognitive attention" (Goffman 1964, 135). Let's unpack this complex definition.

A reference encounter, that is, an encounter that occurs at a library reference desk between a librarian and library user,[2] consists of more than talk about a reference question. It is also the place where and the means by which the participants develop an orientation to one other. They mutually agree to single each other out as the focus of attention, to orient their behavior to one another, and away from other persons and distractions that may be in the immediate environment. This focus, this attention, must be constantly maintained throughout the encounter by the successful establishment and maintenance of what Goffman refers to as "a little system of mutually ratified and ritually governed face-to-face action" Goffman 1964, 136). As described by Watzlawick, Beavin Bavelas, and Jackson (1967), the participants in the encounter will engage in an organized and systematic interplay of action that not only exchanges information through speech, but also maintains the integrity of the conversation. For example, speech in the encounter is overlaid with nonverbal gestures, both large and small, whose purpose is to keep the activity of speaking itself going. Everything at hand is used systematically:

posture, eye-gaze, the intonation of the voice, distance, touch, facial expression, and so on. Once a state of talk has been ratified by the participants in the encounter, nonverbal cues are used to request the floor for speaking, to give up the floor, to inform the other person that attention is being maintained, and to ensure that the conversation proceeds smoothly.

The significance of these nonverbal cues are demonstrated powerfully in a simple exercise involving eye-gaze. Imagine yourself in conversation with another person. You are speaking normally. Now, imagine having that same conversation after you have been instructed to stare directly into the other person's eyes without breaking away. What will happen is that you and the other person will feel uncomfortable very quickly. In polite company, looking directly into the other person's eyes for long periods of time is not considered socially acceptable, and for good reasons. There are generally two social situations in which a person might stare deeply into the eyes of another. The first is intimacy. Looking deeply into the eyes of a loved one communicates an exaggeration of attention, and is therefore a signal of intimacy, especially if the other person willingly returns that gaze. It signifies that the other person is the only object of attention for that time. The other extreme situation is threat. Staring is a signal of hostility, of telling the other to back down. The first person who "blinks" is the loser. In either of these situations, the length of eye-gaze is a very powerful indicator of the context and the relationship of the two people involved, and is reserved for only the most extreme of situations, either extreme intimacy or extreme threat. Otherwise, such staring behavior is seldom seen.

Now imagine carrying on the same conversation, but now you have been instructed not to look at the other person at all, and the other person has been instructed not to look at you. You can look at the floor, the ceiling, or perhaps somewhere to the side of the other person's face, but you are not allowed to look at the other person's face or eyes for any length of time. How does this behavior frame and inform the social situation? Again, you would find it difficult to converse under these conditions. The little system has been compromised. There are technical difficulties; for instance, turn-taking becomes more problematic. One person may talk for longer periods because he cannot receive feedback that the other person wishes to take the floor. However, more important than these is that the participants feel a lack of attention from the other person. Remember Goffman's definition of the encounter: "An environment of mutual monitoring possibilities anywhere within which an individual will find himself accessible to the naked senses of all others who are 'present' and similarly find themselves accessible to him" (Goffman 1964, 135). When eye-gaze and eye contact is withheld in this way, the participants are no longer directly "accessible to the naked senses" of the other. One feels that the other person is not paying attention to her. Talking is difficult because each believes that the other person is not interested. Participants may try to compensate for the lack of eye contact by exaggerating head nods and facial expressions, but if the other person is not looking, these gestures are for naught. So not only does the speaker feel the listener is not paying attention, the listener also feels that the speaker is not paying attention to his feedback. Interestingly, both participants are perfectly capable of hearing what the other person has to say. They can hear the words, the sentences, and utterances. They can hear and understand the *content* of these utterances. Information transfer through speech is not compromised at all. However, the *experience* of having the conversation is severely compromised. When conversations are manipulated by researchers asking people to look at each other too much or too little, it becomes clear that the conversation is now a very different and sometimes extremely difficult experience. In one case, the participants are giving each other too much attention, and in the other case, too little attention. This exercise reveals that a smooth conversation needs an amount of eye contact that is somewhere in the middle--not too much (intimacy/threat), and not too little (disinterest).

In a normal FtF encounter, eye contact is systematically regulated and coordinated. We may not be aware that such coordination is going on. We tend to become aware of it when a regulation has been violated ("Look at me when I'm speaking to you"). We have to look at each other to communicate our attention, but not for too long, so we must look away when the attention is too much. But we do not look away for too long, because this will communicate a lack of attention; therefore, we have to look back, and so on. Both participants engage in an eye-contact dance, for want of a better term, whereby attention is given and taken away to maintain just the right amount of attention and intimacy appropriate for the relationship of the participants.

Another example that plays out at many FtF reference-desk encounters occurs when the library user initiates or takes a cell phone call, reads text messages or scans Facebook posts while in the middle of a reference encounter. Many librarians have asked the authors about this. Librarians feel that this is a face threat and that their time, and that of others who may be waiting, is not being respected. They consider this to be rude, and they often feel at a loss as to how to stop this behavior. Some libraries have put up signs restricting all cell-phone use, or relegating it to the cyber café or lobby. Goffman writes that "face-to-face interaction has its own regulations, it has its own processes and its own structure, and these don't seem to be intrinsically linguistic in character" (Goffman 1964, 136). As we have seen with the eye-contact and cell-phone examples, any linguistic message is always qualified and modified by other simultaneous behaviors, all of which have their own message value. In a conversation, there is never one single message.

In the preceding discussion we have established that the reference encounter is a complex situation that has many dimensions, whether in FtF or virtual modes. We next explore the additional complexities of virtual encounters.

Virtual Encounters

There is ample evidence that as information-seeking has moved towards web-based information sources, more people are seeking the help of librarians via chat or other virtual means (Nicol and Crook 2012). Younger users especially embrace live chat as familiar, convenient, and less intimidating than FtF reference (Radford and Connaway 2007). As technology changes and many types of social and goal-directed interactions become increasingly mediated, the shift in how interpersonal or professional communication takes place may herald a new era of reference encounters. As Rainie and Wellman (2012) point out, smart technology and other forms of electronic communication are radically changing the way we communicate. Some electronic forms of interaction, such as chat, instant messaging, and texting, pose constraints on the amount of information that can be communicated. These forms of mediated technology often do not offer the resources to communicate nonverbally, or the space or time available for maintaining traditional methods of face-work. Anyone who uses texting knows that the greeting and closing rituals are almost always skipped entirely. Also, in this time of ubiquitous global communications, research has shown that closing rituals are not always present in all cultures (Ito and Okabe 2006; Spagnolli and Gamberini 2007; Spilioti 2011; Thurlow and Poff 2011). Could the growth of technology and the increasing exchange of communication and interaction being carried out in mediated formats lead to a less appreciation for the reference encounter? Are more instances of miscommunication inevitable in these contexts?

Computer-mediated communication (CMC) modes, such as chat, lack physical presence and, as discussed in chapter 4, are missing the nonverbal cues, such as facial expressions, tone of voice, or eye contact, that are present in FtF encounters. Communication theorists, such as Watzlawick, Beavin Bavelas, and Jackson (1967), assert that much of the relational work inherent in face-work is communicated nonverbally. Walther (2007) has found, however, that the lack of resources to communicate nonverbal cues in CMC interactions means that individuals are finding ways to compensate by utilizing language-based, rather than nonverbal, strategies to fulfill their relational goals. Essentially individuals develop their relational connections in online conversations through the ways they communicate about the subjects they are discussing (Walther,

Loh, and Granka 2005). However, this seems to be most accurate when people expect relationship development to be necessary because of their expectation of ongoing interactions in the future (Walther et al. 2010)

But what happens when, as in chat reference, interactions have time constraints and participants have no relational goals or do not anticipate any future interactions? It is possible that in online reference situations these limitations might sometimes lead to inattention or quick replies in which one or both people involved do not realize the importance of politeness and other relational work that might make the interaction more successful, as seen in the Physics/Bumper Car example in chapter 5?

This model takes into consideration all of these context variables, including mode, situation, and participant characteristics, which help us to understand the relational work that needs to be accomplished regardless of whether we are involved in FtF or online reference work. Next, we will explain the components of the model that lead to perceptions of success and lack of success, and two types of mixed results that make up the four quadrants.

COMPONENTS OF THE MODEL: CONTENT DIMENSIONS AND RELATIONAL DIMENSIONS

Underneath the circular part of the model are two boxes, one listing content dimensions, one listing relational dimensions (see figure 6.2).

FIGURE 6.2

Content Dimensions and Relational Dimensions

CONTENT DIMENSIONS

Reported Successful +

- Information Access
- Accuracy of Information
- Impact of Technology
- Demonstratable Knowledge
- Appropriate Instruction
- Timeliness of Access

Reported Unsuccessful −

RELATIONAL DIMENSIONS

Reported Successful +

- Attitude
- Relational Quality
- Approachability
- Impact of Technology
- Familiarity
- Greeting Ritual
- Closing Ritual

Reported Unsuccessful −

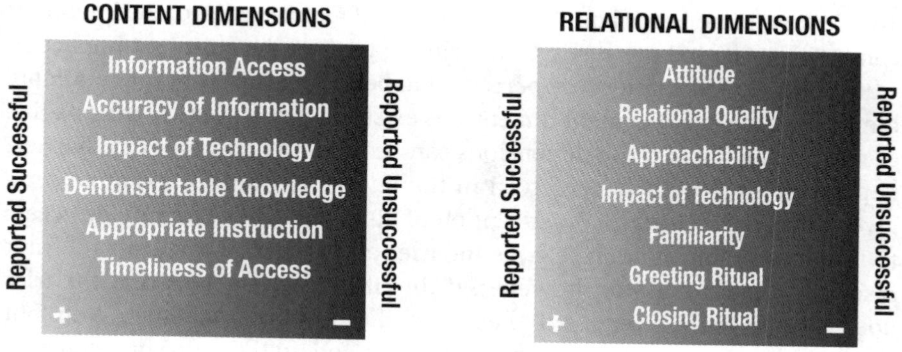

Created by Marie L. Radford and Lynn Silipigni Conaway. © 2015 Marie L. Radford and OCLC

These boxes are integral to the model because they contain factors that have been painstakingly identified as critical to perceptions of success, lack of success, and mixed results. Through many years of research, the authors and their colleagues have collected a large amount of data from reference encounter participants as well as verbatim VRS session transcripts that have informed the development of this model. The model rests on a finely detailed category scheme of relational and content dimensions that includes facilitators as well as barriers to success. Facilitators are "qualities or characteristics that have a positive impact on the perceptions of the participants in the interaction" (Radford 1999, 50). On the other hand, barriers are "qualities or characteristics that had a negative impact on the perceptions of the participants" (Radford 1999, 59). These categories were initially constructed by Radford (1993, 1999), who focused her investigation on FtF interactions, and conducted observations and in-depth interviews with librarians and library users. Radford (2006a) expanded and refined these categories in a study of live chat transcripts. Over the course of two large Institute for Museum and Library Services (IMLS) grant-funded projects (Radford and Connaway 2005–2008; Radford, Connaway, and Shah 2011–2014), additional research included library users who did not use live chat reference (VRS) and users of web-based Social Q & A (SQA) services (such as Yahoo! Answers). These large-scale projects included focus groups, interviews, surveys, transcript analysis, and design sessions that further applied and expanded the authors' understanding of how people made decisions about the success of their encounters. This research was able to define and illustrate numerous relational and content facilitators and barriers to success, as discussed below.

Content Dimensions

The Content Dimensions box shown in figure 6.2 features a list of the important content aspects that our research has shown to have the strongest impact on whether or not encounters are perceived to be successful. As in the relational dimension, the list of content dimensions exists on a continuum from positive to negative. Each of these dimensions can be either a facilitator or a barrier, depending on how it is perceived in the encounter. So, for example, in a given encounter a librarian's perception of his or her ability to provide access to the needed information (e.g., is the user able to get to the most relevant resources) is a facilitator; however, if the librarian perceives that the user does not have access (e.g., only has the ability to search the open Web, but not the subscription databases, and is unable to get to the relevant resources) this lack of access is viewed as having a negative impact.

Content Facilitators

Content facilitators are information-related aspects of an encounter that have positive impacts on the librarian-user interaction and that enhance communication, which contributes to success in reference service encounters (see also Radford 1999, 2006a). These include:

- Providing information access (Was other person enabled to use resources?)
- Providing accurate information (Was correct information/instruction provided?)
- Providing specific information (Was exact question answered with requested detail?)
- Demonstrating general or specialized knowledge (Did the other person demonstrate understanding and knowledge of topic and/or library systems?)
- Giving appropriate instruction (Was instruction provided if needed? Was level and depth right?)
- Providing convenient/timely access (Was access prompt, given constraints on staff time and resources? Were any barriers that occurred easily overcome?)

Content Barriers

In contrast to facilitators, content barriers are information-related aspects that have negative impact on the librarian-user interaction and that impede communication, contributing to lack of success in reference-service encounters (see also Radford 1999, 2006a). These include:

- No access to information (Was access unavailable or restricted?)
- Inaccuracy (Was information incorrect, biased, or out-of-date?)
- Negative impact of technology (Did technology hinder encounter?)
- Lack of general or specialized knowledge (Was the other person unable to demonstrate needed knowledge or skills?)
- Lack of appropriate instruction (Was there insufficient, overly complex, or excessively detailed instruction?)
- Unrealistic task (Was there not enough time to address the task? Was the need impossible to fulfill?)

Relational Dimensions

Let's take a closer look at the Relational Dimensions box in figure 6.2. It provides a list of the important relational aspects that our research has shown to have the strongest impact on whether or not encounters are perceived to be successful. Within the relational dimension, we found that these aspects exist on a continuum from positive to negative; each of these can be either a facilitator or a barrier, depending on how it is perceived in the encounter. So for example, in a given encounter a librarian's perception of positive attitude on the part of the user (e.g., outlook about the task at hand) is a facilitator; however, if the librarian perceives that the user has a negative attitude, it is viewed as having a negative impact.

Relational Facilitators

Within the realm of relational dimension, relational facilitators are interpersonal aspects of an encounter that have a positive impact on the librarian- user interaction and enhance communication. A large amount of research evidence over many years confirms that their presence in encounters greatly contributes to perceptions of successful reference service encounters (see also Radford 1999, 2006a). Examples of these include:

- Positive attitude (Is the other friendly? Interested? Willing to help?)
- Positive relationship quality (Is a good rapport established?)
- Approachability (Is it easy to engage the other? Is eye contact/word contact made?)
- Positive impact of technology (Does use of computer or online resources help?)
- Familiarity (Has a previous encounter with this person been successful?)
- Greeting ritual (Did the other say hello or give another acknowledgment?)
- Closing ritual (Did the other end with a pleasant good-bye?)

Radford (2006a) found that interpersonal aspects are particularly vital to perceptions of success on the part of VRS users. This may be attributable to the text-based nature of VRS, in which the absence of some of the nonverbal and verbal cues present in FtF situations, or when a busy service can result in the librarian's attention being divided among more than one user (remember the Physics/Bumper Car example from chapter 4?). Some interpersonal strategies include:

- Rapport building (Is an effort made to establish a personal relationship, or is the encounter cut and dried or robotic?)
- Compensation for lack of nonverbal cues (Are emoticons, emojis, or text, such as the spelling out of nonverbal behaviors, such as "ha ha" or <smile>, used appropriately?)
- Strategies for relationship development (Do the participants share in self-disclosure, provide encouragement, etc.?)
- Evidence of deference and respect (Are participants polite?)
- Face-saving tactics (Are apologies given when appropriate? Do participants agree to try what has been suggested?)
- Greeting and closing rituals (These are even more important in VRS than in FtF communication, because they work to establish a human connection, as opposed to search-engine-like presence and can prevent negative outcomes, like abrupt log off.)

As might be expected, Radford (2006a) also found that VRS users showed more deference to librarians (using polite expressions, agreeing to try what is suggested, etc.) than librarians did to users, after a close look at the chat transcripts. This result was also found by Radford and Connaway (2007) who discovered that younger users (especially those below college level, who librarians perceive to have homework questions) were not treated with as much deference as more mature users. To achieve success, especially with younger users, respect and face-work are essential. Younger users soon grow up and become college students and parents, so it is vital that they have good experiences in both FtF and VRS encounters all along the way.

Relational Barriers

As opposed to facilitators, relational barriers are the opposite side of the continuum. They are interpersonal aspects that have negative impact on the librarian-client interaction and that impede communication. These contribute to lack of success in reference service encounters (see also Radford 1999, 2006a). Examples include:

- Negative attitude (Is the other angry? Impatient? Stern? Disrespectful?)
- Negative relational quality (Is poor rapport evident? Are there misunderstandings that are not repaired in the course of the encounter?)
- Lack of approachability (Is the other person reluctant to engage?)
- Negative impact of technology (Does use of computer or online resources detract? Are there problems with the software, systems, or VRS interface?)

- Absence of greeting ritual (Was there no hello or acknowledgment?)
- Lack of closing ritual (Was there an abrupt end, without any good-bye?)

Also, participant/characteristics make a difference to perceptions of barriers as well. Radford (2006a) found that VRS users exhibit barriers (e.g., rudeness, impatience) that differ greatly from those of librarians (e.g., negative closure, limiting time, reprimands).

Each of the four quadrants of the model (or pieces of the pie) represent possible outcomes for an encounter: perceptions of successful outcome, perceptions of unsuccessful outcome, mixed results positive content (negative relational), and mixed results positive relational (negative content). To explain the model more thoroughly, some examples for each of the four quadrants follow.

FIGURE 6.3

Perceptions of Successful Outcome Quadrant

Created by Marie L. Radford and Lynn Silipigni Connaway. © 2015 Marie L. Radford and OCLC

Perceptions of Successful Outcome Quadrant: Both the Content and Relational Needs Are Perceived as Having Been Met

In the Successful quadrant, as shown in figure 6.3, both the content and relational dimensions of the reference encounter are perceived as being successful by the user and/or the librarian. The user has received the information or instruction he or she needs and felt comfortable and happy with the communication that has taken place. The librarian has provided the appropriate information or instruction, and has also felt comfortable with the communication that has taken place. Examples that illustrate this quadrant follow.

Interactions classified as belonging to the Successful quadrant are characterized by reports such as this one from a library user's online survey from the Seeking Synchronicity grant project (Radford and Connaway 2005–2008). The library user describes both success in the interpersonal aspects as well as in finding information and achieving a positive outcome of an "A" on a paper.

> The Librarian was very easy to work with and she or he was able to understand and was well able to handle my question. [VRS name] is Awesome!!!! I was having difficulties finding information on weather related instrumentation and [VRS name] helped me locate this information for me to gain an A on my paper. Also I received a backup e-mail from my college librarian and she was able to continue the flow of information for me to complete my research paper. (User Online Survey-20336)

To get an idea of the Successful quadrant from the librarian's point of view, we have two examples from librarians who were interviewed for the Cyber Synergy grant project (Radford, Connaway, and Shah 2011–2014). They were asked to recall and describe an online reference encounter that they considered successful. Here's the first one:

> A girl came in on VR Chat, asking about Lord of the Rings and mentioned that she wanted to learn Elvish. I happened to know that there [are] resources online and print that I could recommend. She just sort of mentioned it in passing, when I showed an interest in helping she got very excited. She was embarrassed and I could reassure her that there were resources, it was a legitimate question and I could help her out. i really sort of realized that there is no such thing as wasted knowledge. I know a lot about constructed languages it makes you feel good. No matter where you learn things there is that practical application in reference work. (Librarian Interview 16)

One of the interesting things about this example from Librarian 16 is that the user was embarrassed about her question regarding Elvish. The librarian addresses the user's self-disclosure directly through a willingness to reassure her that this was a legitimate question. It is possible to see that this encounter could have gone the other way if the librarian had no subject knowledge about constructed languages, or had not taken the question seriously (as in our Physics/Bumper Car example in chapter 5).

Here's another example from Cyber Synergy:

> The one that comes to mind is a question that began as an e-mail. It was from a distance student in one of our really successful programs for integrated marketing communications. The student needed to find consumer information about Volkswagen and sales . . . just everything about Volkswagen; they were trying to pull together a report. I began by sending back some instructions for accessing data in the Mediamark Reporter, the person wrote back, and then it turned into a variety of difficulties he was having. He couldn't get remote access to the data; we ended up with several phone calls. He was employed full time, so we had a phone call when I was at home and I used a new website software . . . I wish I could tell you what it was . . . it's a website like a screen sharing device but you can do it on the fly. On the phone, I showed him how to do the research in this particular database and save it into a spreadsheet and format the spreadsheet. It was kind of fantastic! He was really pleased at the end and it was so nice to be able to have a phone conversation. Seems to me that folks are less and less inclined to phone us than to text, but some of these interactions are so complex with chat, but so simple on the phone, especially with screen sharing as we talked our way through the process. That's one that stands out. He expressed his wonderment at the wonderful data he had access to and his gratitude for the time we spent together. It was a pretty long interaction; we were on the phone for more than an hour. Some of these distance classes I do make some good inroads and get to do some good virtual interactions, but some I don't get much traction from the professors. Distance students don't always end up finding out about some of the resources that suit their needs. I felt like I really made a connection with the guy and helped him succeed in his class. (Librarian Interview 20)

The preceding example from Librarian 20 illustrates the ways in which reference encounters are merging and morphing from one mode to another. This one starts out as an e-mail and ends up as a phone call. The librarian goes the extra mile for this user, calling him from home because he was a distance student who was working full time. The librarian says that the user expressed "wonderment" and "gratitude." The librarian states that she made a personal "connection" and helped him to "succeed in his class." Here we can see the combination of information/instruction given as well as relational engagement.

How are the content and relational needs met in a virtual live-chat interaction? The Marine Mammals transcript from the Cyber Synergy grant project (Radford, Connaway, and Shah 2011–2014) provides another illuminating illustration of this quadrant. As you read it, notice how both the information/instruction needs are met, and also how a positive relationship is developed in the flow of the session. Note that grammatical or spelling errors have not been corrected to preserve the verbatim text.

Successful Outcome Quadrant Transcript Example: Marine Mammals

Question typed into query box: I am having trouble finding articles of the evolution of marine mammals?

1. Librarian (L) Hi
2. User (U) Hi
3. L So, you need journal articles that talk about the evolution of marine mammals. What have you tried so far?
4. U i have tried online databases through my home university, my professor says there is recent research but i cannot find it . . . ive looked specifically with scienedirect but no luck
5. L Okay. Can you tell me a little about the assignment? As in, how recent does your professor want the research to be . . . what your particular focus is, etc.
6. U Sure, I am writing a paper on the evolution of marine mammals from terrestrial origin and then change back to the sea. I am specifically interested in the connection between manatees and their relative the Dugong who lives in Australia . . . I'm pretty sure the professor doesnt need it to be very recent research, he said the newest stuff was put out about 20 yrs ago . . .
7. L (I love manatees! I think they are cute) . . . Okay . . . back to your research :)
8. U they are soo cute and really ancient which maks them evern more interesting!

9	L	Neat! I cannot access the databases through your library because a password has not been provided, but we have
10	L	. . . databases at my library
11	L	Have you tried searching in Academic Search Premier? It is not "science specific" but it is user friendly. I can work through Academic Search Complete at the same time and we can see what we can find. Okay?
12	U	is that a journal?
13	L	It is a database through which you can find journal articles.
14	U	would i have access through my home university or should i just google it?
15	U	oh i found it!
16	L	Good! Did you find it through your library's home page?
17	U	yes, its listed as one of their databases
18	U	would you recommend using marine mammals and ecolution as the key terms? i always seem to use the wrong key terms . . .
19	L	Okay. I am in Academic Search Complete and I entered the word "manatees" in the first box and "evolution" in the second box. I also limited the search to Academic (peer reviewed) journals. I received 15 articles back. What do you get with these search terms?
20	U	im not sure where to select peer reviewed journal articles
21	U	nevermind haha i found it
22	L	:)
23	L	I broadened the search a bit. I entered Marine mammals as a "subject" term and received 550 articles. (The 15 I received from searching for manatees seemed to be very specific and very scientific, but they may be just what you are looking for.)
24	U	yes, the 15 i got were a little to specific becuase im looking for a great understanding of the whole story as well as some specific changes, ill broden the search again
25	L	Try "Marine Mammals" as a subject term in the first line (you may have to use the drop-down menu to select "subject") and then "evolution" in the second box but leave it as "select a field" or the general search. Do any of those articles look helpful?
26	L	Remember also that you can skim an article and find who that author quotes. It is a good way to broaden the search and find more resources.
27	U	there are a couple that look helpful, it is so hard to find an artical that covers a big topic, im wondering if books will be more helpful for the big picture stuff and articles for the specifics?

28	L	That's a good idea. It all depends upon what sources your professor says you can use. Sometimes encyclopedia articles are also helpful, especially for the "big picture" (not wikipedia, of course!)
29	U	haha yea not wikipedia, although it is a good place to find other links and articles where they list references, some are from journals and you can work backwards . . .
30	L	True!
31	L	I am now in Science Direct, which (in my opinion) is a little less user-friendly but it does have good resources. I tried entering "marine mammals" in the "All fields" box and after getting those results, entering "evolution" in the "Search within results" box and then selecting Limit to Journal. There are still 14,672 articles. I will see if I can limit it some
32	L	Is any of this helping?
33	U	yes it is! i think i found an article, but im nott sure if its an entire pdf . . . im trying to see if i can find it
34	L	Okay. I will keep searching Science Direct for now and tell you what I find and how I find it.
35	U	thanks so much!!
36	L	I discovered that in Science Direct you should put "marine mammals" in quotation marks in the search box so it will search for both terms together.
37	L	Did you find the pdf article yet?
38	U	ohhhh ok . . . and no it just keeps re-routing me to other places where the full text could be . . . if i give you the citation so you think you could find the full text?
39	L	I could try. What is the title of the article and the author's name?
40	U	Holden, Constance. "Fishy missing link?" Science 314.5802 (2006): 1057. General OneFile. Web. 15 Oct. 2010.
41	L	Okay.
42	L	Also, in Science Direct, when I selected the "search" link, I was able to enter "marine mammals" and "evolution" as Keyword searches and came up with 3 articles.
43	U	ok ill try that next
44	L	Still working on it . . .
45	U	me too! i really appreciate your help!
46	L	You are welcome! This is an elusive article. Someone is helping me try to get the full-text.
47	U	i agree its like its not even a article just an abstract! i hate that!
48	U	i agree its like its not even a article just an abstract! i hate that!

49	L	It seems that the abstract might be all we have access to. Does your library have a subscription to the journal "Science" for November 2006?
50	U	thats what im trying to find out . . . just one minute
51	U	i think we doo. .
52	U	it says i can find the article through all these other databases . . . but none of them fgive me the full text
53	L	Good! I know. It is frustrating. (It is frustrating us, too!) Usually it will not provide the link to another database unless that database contains the full text.
54	L	If you talk with a librarian at your library and discover they do not have a subscription, you can order the article through interlibrary loan.
55	L	Do you think you have enough information now to continue your search?
56	U	ok. . it think ill just keep the citation and try monday on capus to get the article becuas ei can read others online
57	U	That sounds like a good plan!
58	L	Is there anything else I can help you with?
59	U	yes i think ido! are there any other databases that you would recommend to look in>
60	L	I would try Science Direct again, and the hints I listed above. All databases (except those specified for business or something) should have links to some articles. I just tried Academic OneFile and did an Advanced search for keywords "marine mammals" and "evolution" and limited the search to peer-reviewed and full-text and came up with 8 articles. I think looking for books in the library might also be a good idea, if your professor will allow books as a
61	L	When we close the chat, you will get a copy of the conversation if you provided your e-mail address when you opened the chat.
62	U	i think he will allow books, ill e-mail him and find out . . . thanks so much for all of your help, it was definitely beneifical! have a great weekend! :)
63	L	Thank you! You have a great weekend, too!
64	L	[It has been a pleasure chatting with you. Thank you for using [service name]!]

In the flow of this virtual encounter, with its back-and-forth of turn-taking, it is clear that success can be seen in both the establishment of good rapport and the successful provision of instruction and information. Right from the beginning, the librarian chooses not to use any prepared scripts, and opts for the informal greeting ritual in line 1, "Hi," to which the user replies in line 2 with "Hi." This initial greeting sets up a positive vibe for the encounter that continues throughout. Interestingly, no scripted responses are contained in this transcript until the closing in line 64.

The success of the relational dimension is further highlighted in lines 7 and 8, and again in lines 20 to 22. In line 7, note the librarian's comment "(I love manatees! I think they are cute) . . . Okay . . . back to your research :)" that gives some self-disclosure—that the librarian loves manatees—as well as a smiley emoticon :) that is, of course, a textual representation of a smile. The user responds in line 8 "they are soo cute and really ancient which maks [sic] them evern [sic] more interesting!" which is an appropriate response to the librarian and helps to create a very positive tone that lasts for the entire encounter. Soon, in lines 20 to 22, this exchange takes place. In line 20, the user says "im not sure where to select peer reviewed journal articles," but in line 21 the user says, somewhat playfully "nevermind haha i found it." The librarian replies in acknowledgment of the playful tone with a smiley face in line 22 ":)" to further build rapport. Additional relational work is found in lines 52 and 53, where the librarian agrees with the user that the inability to locate full text can be frustrating. This exemplifies empathy, a strong relational facilitator that encourages rapport development on the part of the librarian.

On the content side, the *Science* article the user mentions is elusive; however, the librarian provides instruction throughout the session in a nonthreatening way, especially in teaching the user how to find subject information, in this case specifically on marine mammals. In lines 25 and 26 instruction is given in how to search the database and how to find background information. The comments about Wikipedia are interesting: the librarian says "(not Wikipedia)," but the user replies that this website can be helpful at times, and the librarian confirms this idea in line 30 by saying "True!" This exchange is a good example of deference from librarian to user. The librarian confirms that the user's view of Wikipedia is appropriate. A face threat is avoided here, because the librarian could have easily been disconfirming to the user by a statement like "Wikipedia should never be used." Further instruction is given in line 36 (on how to use quotation marks in ScienceDirect), and in line 60, where the librarian suggests a search strategy that includes looking in specific databases as well as in books. The closing ritual that begins with line 57 is a good example of the way in which a successful ending can be accomplished in live chat. The librarian reassures the user that he or she will get a transcript of the session, and suggests additional database to check. Pleasantries are exchanged, and in line 62 the user says thank you. It is clear that both parties are pleased with this encounter, even though the article in *Science* was not immediately available. Excellent rapport development and the amount of instruction provided characterize this encounter as successful. Throughout the session, a positive and professional tone is used and both parties have expressed satisfaction.

Perceptions of Unsuccessful Outcome Quadrant: Both the Content and Relational Needs Are Perceived as Not Having Been Met

In the Unsuccessful quadrant (as shown in figure 6.4) neither relational nor content needs are met. For example, the library user may not have received the information or instruction he or she or she desired, and he or she may also have had a bad experience interacting with the librarian. From the viewpoint of the librarian, information/instruction was not provided and the encounter was unpleasant. Failures for both dimensions result in interactions in this quadrant to be perceived as unsuccessful.

FIGURE 6.4

Perceptions of Unsuccessful Outcome Quadrant

Created by Marie L. Radford and Lynn Silipigni Connaway. © 2015 Marie L. Radford and OCLC

The following example is from a library user's online survey from the Seeking Synchronicity grant project (Radford and Connaway 2005–2008). The user's query about the location of a book was not satisfactorily answered, and the librarian was perceived as "not being very helpful." This is a classic example of "negative closure" where the user perceives that the librarian is offering less help than needed (see Ross and Dewdney 1998).

> I once asked a librarian when I was in the library where a certain book was and she said "oh I think its [sic] over in that section." She didn't help me find it and she wasn't positive of even where it was. She sent me in the correct direction but, did not further help me to actually find the book and was not positive of if it was even there and gave me no details of how to find it. I don't think it had to do with being face-to-face I think it had to do with her not being very helpful. (VRS Non-User Online Survey-37830)

The following example from the Cyber Synergy interviews shows the librarian's viewpoint. The librarian describes a critical incident centering on a science question. He or she feels that the encounter was not successful for content/information given or on the relational level.

> I recently had a question regarding a phylum of a fungi. The student couldn't communicate to me what about this fungus she needed to know. She said she wanted it general, but kept referring to Google searches. When I located articles that started to indicate this was a class of fungus she was looking for, she exhibited that she was really frustrated with what was going on because I couldn't specifically identify what she was looking for. I verified the spelling, then went to one of our biology encyclopedias to attempt to find what the word meant. Unfortunately the student couldn't communicate what I needed to know to do an accurate search for her, and had a condescending reaction without recognizing that with a search strategy, you have to start with one concept to build the next concept. My barrier was my lack of knowledge plus my lack of jargon and it created an almost impassable situation where I could just give her suggestions on how to search and point her to reference books with the most general biology and fungus information. What I should have done was when I first recognized that this was a biological term was use one of our open access sources and put in the word to come up with a quick understanding instead of trying to teach myself what I was looking for. If I had just stopped and recognized what this was, I could have gone to this other source with a generic definition

and gone from there to reassure her we were doing something useful. I decided to handle the question this way because it's kind of standard, just scan as quickly as you can and try and absorb it. Unfortunately, if they're all words you don't understand, the science databases were full of huge sciency jargon. Also, because I was unable to conduct a reference interview with the student because she was really reluctant to share the information I needed, it shifted too quickly for me to catch up. This particular patron is one who repeatedly comes to the desk and doesn't want to absorb search strategies, so learning is absent from the interaction . . . but I'll keep trying! (Librarian Interview 35)

The librarian is quite sympathetic to the user and it is notable that this is a user who the librarian is familiar with since she "repeatedly comes to the desk." It is admirable that the librarian tried hard and is willing to "keep trying!" rather than give up on this user. The librarian feels that the user was not forthcoming and states that "she was really reluctant to share the information I needed," and also notes that the user's minimal science vocabulary contributed to the failure of the encounter.

We have already shared an example from the Unsuccessful quadrant in the infamous Physics/Bumper Car transcript in chapter 5. In that transcript, the interpersonal relationship was full of face threats and indirect shaming ("Is this a homework question?") and the user's question was never answered. Here is a second example from the Seeking Synchronicity grant project (Radford and Connaway 2005–2008). This transcript is short but very telling. The user's question may be one that does not have a scientific response, but this encounter is totally unsuccessful on both content and relational levels. As you read this transcript, notice how the librarian fails to engage the user in any question negotiation, and does not take steps to establish a personal relationship. Additionally, the librarian also fails to provide any useable answer or content.

Unsuccessful Quadrant Transcript Example: Telekinetic Powers

Question typed into query box: I want to learn how to have telekinetic powers

1	U	I want to learn how to have telekinetic powers
2	L	[A librarian will be with you in about a minute.]
3	L	[Librarian [Name]—A librarian has joined the session.]

4	L	will be things about it, but may not tell you how to do it
5	L	"telekinetic powers" gets 19,000 hits in google–
6	L	adding site:edu gets 141—mostly things about stories that talk about it
7	L	"telekinesis" site:edu gets 1900
8	U	I HATE THIS WEBSITE AND I WILL NEVER COME HERE AGAIN
9	U	[patron—has disconnected]

Rather than beginning with a greeting ritual, the librarian starts out with two impersonal and scripted responses in lines 2 and 3, and then a face threat in line 4 in the form of a disclaimer "will be things about it, but may not tell you how to do it." This is followed by the librarian stating what search terms he or she entered in Google, and the numbers of hits. Because a personal relationship is not established in the early part of this session, it is not surprising that disaster is lurking ahead.

It is possible that the librarian could have used a lighter touch (e.g., "I would like to have telekinetic powers myself :))" or even "this is an interesting question, let me see what I can find, although my guess is that I won't find a scientific approach to what you are looking for"). A softer touch could have led to more relational success, even if the question is unanswerable. The user is not present in the encounter until line 8, where we see the user flame the librarian with all caps: "I HATE THIS WEBSITE AND I WILL NEVER COME HERE AGAIN." This is followed by an abrupt disconnect, which reveals a very high level of frustration on the part of the user. This transcript is fascinating, because it shows how important starting with a greeting and establishing a personal relationship with the user is in achieving some level of success. By logging off abruptly, an act that Goffman (1967) would call an avoidance strategy, the user gives the librarian no opportunity to react to the frustration or to repair the face threats. The librarian did not address the relational side of this virtual encounter, remaining fully centered in the content dimension and performing the search without realizing the level of face threat that the cold (and arguably robotic) type of response was presenting to the user. The authors have spoken to science librarians about this encounter. They have responded with "this is an absurd question," and believe that the librarian was justified in making the disclaimer in line 4 and to not taking the question seriously, because it is not scientifically possible to have telekinetic powers. What do you think? Would the user be likely to return to this service the next time he or she has an information need? Would a softer touch be advisable or desirable?

Mixed Results—Relational Successful Quadrant: Contents Needs Are Not Met but Relational Needs are Met

In the Mixed Results—Relational Successful quadrant shown in figure 6.5, there is good relational development, but there is a problem in the content/information dimension. To illustrate this quadrant, the first example comes from a library user's online survey from the Seeking Synchronicity grant project (Radford and Connaway 2005–2008). Our research has found that content can sometimes take a back seat to interpersonal communication in perceptions of success, especially for users. This may be difficult for librarians to believe, but many users report that an encounter was successful despite the fact that they did not get the information (in this case location of a video) requested. This user liked the librarian using her name, which was also found to be true in many cases in interviews and focus groups that the authors and colleagues have done over many years, especially from the viewpoint of younger users. This user felt that he or she had "received special treatment," underlining the importance of the personal touch.

FIGURE 6.5

Mixed Results—Relational Successful Quadrant

Created by Marie L. Radford and Lynn Silipigni Connaway. © 2015 Marie L. Radford and OCLC

> I attempted to locate the video, unsuccessfully; during the search I stumbled on the [VRS name] resource, and utilized it. We, the librarian and I, were unsuccessful in locating the copy but she did a great job in her search. The quick, to the point conversation, was very warm, intimate, so fast and she used my name. I liked that. I appreciated the service of pulling up websites for me, right before my eyes! She understood my request. She explained what she was doing. She mentioned a few times "I'm still searching." My patience would grow for she was so nice. I just knew she would be able to help me. We didn't find the video, but the exchange was successful. Also to tell the truth, I felt I received special treatment even though every chat user has this experience. (User Online Survey-90021)

From the viewpoint of the user, he or she did not receive the needed information, but is nevertheless satisfied with the interpersonal qualities of the interaction itself. The user may feel that the librarian treated him or her well, even if desired information or instruction was not provided. Similarly, from the viewpoint of the librarian, the information dimension might be deemed to be unsuccessful (the correct information was not found or appropriate instruction was not provided), but the relational development was satisfactory.

Here's an example from the librarian's point of view from the Cyber Synergy project to further illustrate this quadrant:

> This was a virtual chat question and the person said that they were trying to find things that were about the Israeli-Palestinian conflict and how to tell whether or not that particular journal article or book had presented all the sides of the issue. They needed to read something that discussed the entire scope of the Israeli-Palestinian conflict and that fairly presented both sides. This is a problem in our databases because we don't often label the position or tone or make a distinction about the author's position in their writing. I asked the person to supply some examples because they said they had found some things, and the person supplied a title of a documentary history of the conflict. It was, of course, as a documentary history, provided primary sources and translations. It was published by Oxford University Press, so I tried to assure the person that anything by that press would have presented both sides. Turns out there were no reviews of the book, I think the magazines that are selecting what books to review can't get a review published for every single book. I explained to the person how to look for reviews of other titles. I also consulted with one of the other reference librarians and

she suggested we have a database called Opposing Viewpoints, which is very good because for every view, it provides a list of thesauri that would give you the view for that viewpoint. There was another thing I suggested the person try: an article on an academic journal that looked like it was an overview and I suggested reviewing that journal and its sources to see what are the points that are being discussed. In one way, I recall it as being frustrating because the person came to the realization that they were at the beginning of this search and needed to read one or two things to get a sense of the range of the issues, so I thought that as a very important and positive thing. Part of the reason why I view this as a frustrating reference question is that sometimes the person you're trying to help is not ready to move forward and make these realizations that they need to get some information to see what argument they want to move forward with. Before virtual things, if I had gotten this type of reference question, if I'd had this type of question at the reference desk in earlier days, I would have had them look in an encyclopedia. (Librarian Interview 36)

In this example from the Cyber Synergy project, the librarian makes some suggestions for background reading, but is not able to answer the user's question directly and fully. Through referrals and the suggestions made it is possible that the student will be able to find the needed information, but that remains to be seen. Librarian 36 is frustrated on the content side, because the databases do not "label the position or tone or make a distinction about the author's position in their writing." On the relational side, however, the librarian is able to make a breakthrough in getting the person to realize he or she must exert effort, which the librarian says is "a very important and positive thing." Previous research has found that the user's attitude toward the task and willingness to do the required work are critically important relational facilitators for the librarian (see Radford 2006a).

One more example for this quadrant comes from a Cyber Synergy project transcript that illustrates mixed results, with success on the relational side, but none in the content area.

Mixed Results—Relational Successful Quadrant Transcript Example: E-book Printing

Question typed into query box: how do i view and print out pages from a ebook from my home PC?

1	L	so your having trouble with your ebook platform?
2	U	Yes
3	L	i found some directions for you—please hold
4	U	i found the book i am looking for but i cant open the book
5	L	ok—
6	L	did you connect through 'search ebooks'?
7	U	Yes
8	L	did it take you to netLibrary?
9	L	you don't want that . . .
10	U	thats where it take me
11	L	ok—this seems to be the problem . . .
12	L	let me send you the instructions they have listed . . .
13	U	Ok
14	L	If you click Search eBooks, but are directed to the NetLibrary home page instead of the proxy login screen (or the Harbor College eContent collection page), please clear your browser's cache, close your browser, and open it
15	L	this is their suggestion to resolve this . . .
16	U	let me try that
17	L	do you think you can go through these steps ok?
18	L	{Can I help you with anything else today?}
19	L	HI—I haven't heard from you in awhile. Are you still there?
20	U	i have the book that i wont but it not letting me view the book still
21	L	ok—
22	L	let me get you the phone number at the library to call for tech support—will that work for you?
23	U	[phone number]
24	L	here's the number for the reference desk—they should be able to walk you through it—
25	L	[phone number]
26	L	it's a little different than the one you have—why don't you try this one . . .
27	U	Ok
28	L	my shift is ending but if you'd like more help i can transfer you to another librarian, or you can sign in again—what would you like?
29	U	Yes
30	L	which would you like to do?
31	U	you can transfer me

32   L   LibCloseCOB;

33   L   Instant Message request from librarian: [Lib. 1 Full Name] to librarian: [Lib. 2 Full Name]

34   L2   Hi, give me a sec to look over your question! I be right with you . . .

35   U   thats fine

36   L2   OK, I'm sorry not to have any immediate suggestions—were you able to speak to someone at your library's reference desk yet?

37   U   not yet

38   U   its not 8 yet there not open

39   L2   Oh! Sorry, wasn't thinking since it's already 10 here! Did you try clearing the cache and restarting the browser?

40   U   thank you i have to go to school. yes i tryed doing that

41   L2   I'm sorry—I don't really have any other suggestions . . . hopefully your librarians can clear the matter up for you when the library opens—I'm sorry for not having a solution . . .

42   L2   ChatLibrarianEnded;.

43   L2   ResolutionNote;: RCFollowupByPatronLibrary;

44   L3   Hi [User First Name],Did you get the ebook open? The trick from home is to go through the Netlibrary page directly at [URL] www .netlibrary.com and then logging in with your campus user name and password. Please let me know if you're still having problems with it.

In this example, something that seems like it would be pretty straightforward involves three different librarians trying to assist one user in opening up and printing an e-book. Although the solution appears in line 44, it looks like the user logged off in line 42, so most likely he or she did not receive this information. The transcript will be sent to the user, but it is impossible to tell whether the user was successful in opening and printing needed pages from the e-book. Each of the librarians, however, is relationally polite, offering numerous apologies and abundant inclusion of the user with sincere (if largely futile) attempts to be helpful. In lines 25–27 the librarian is persistent in trying to help, although the user had not responded in a while. Lines 40–42 show one referral, and the last line is the second referral. In reading the encounter in the flow of turn-taking, it can be seen how the unsuccessful content affects the positive relational work; consequently, this encounter has a mixed result, rather than being fully successful.

Mixed Results—Content Successful Quadrant: Content Needs Are Met but Relational Needs Are Not Met

The following example illustrates the Mixed Results—Content Successful quadrant, as shown in figure 6.6. It is from a library user's online survey from the Seeking Synchronicity grant (Radford and Connaway 2005–2008). Here the librarian chose to push an FAQ (Frequently Asked Questions) page designed to answer user questions, which requires some work on the user's part to read through the information. The user was unhappy because there was no personal note, and also because the specific answer was not given quickly and precisely. The comment "some customer service would have been nice" reflects that the encounter was relationally unsuccessful. Pushing general information when users asked for specific information is identified as a barrier to accuracy in VRS (further discussed by Radford and Connaway 2013). This also illustrates that users value the convenience of getting the exact answer, rather than a page that contains the answer (see also Connaway, Dickey, and Radford 2011).

FIGURE 6.6

Mixed Results—Content Successful Quadrant

Created by Marie L. Radford and Lynn Silipigni Connaway. © 2015 Marie L. Radford and OCLC

> One time I wrote in to my public library asking about late fees. I know that's not a research question, but this was the only time I can think of that I had a not-so-great experience. The library just quickly put the link of that info (along with a lot of other info I had to sift through). There was no personal note from the person—just the link, like I said, that I had to sift through. It was just the FAQs of the library. Some customer service would have been nice. If they would have typed "20 cents a day," that would have been much nicer. I felt it was rude. I found the answer, so it ended up ok. Maybe they get lots of extraneous questions like that, so they are annoyed. To me, if you like helping people, it shouldn't matter what they ask. (User Online Survey-73324)

From the user's point of view, the content provided is satisfactory (e.g., he or she has received the desired information or instruction), but nevertheless he or she felt unhappy with the interpersonal qualities of the interaction.

The transcript of the Christian Musical Group encounter from the Cyber Synergy project further illustrates this quadrant. As you read this transcript, which is unusually long, pay attention to the relational dimension. What went wrong here, and why? With younger users, as was seen in the Physics/Bumper Car example in chapter 5, there is a need for some early relational work within the greeting ritual and throughout the encounter. The librarian is professional and does find an answer (even though she cannot provide access to the requested item), but the user's attempts to be polite and deferential, and to establish a personal connection, seem to fall on deaf ears.

Mixed Results—Content Successful Quadrant Transcript Example: Christian Musical Group

Question typed into query box: hi there.i just called [library name] i called them because i cant seem to find this musical group.it's a christian musical group cd.i really want to borrow it.because i want to listen to the songs especially "who am i."i was wondering to see if that library can help to request it so then i can pick it up on [library name].please help me to find some information on that cd.

1	L	What did they say?
2	U	who?
3	L	the library
4	L	the [library name] did they say anthing

5	U	The [library name]?
6	U	no one is answering the phone
7	U	right now
8	L	what is the group
9	U	hold on plz
10	U	it's ringing
11	U	i cant seem to get hold of the library
12	U	the librarian is away from the desk
13	U	so can u plz help me
14	L	Can I have the name of the musical group
15	U	im begging u [Lib. First Name]
16	U	it's called the casting crowns
17	U	scroll to the msg question that i typed
18	U	scroll to the msg question that i typed
19	U	everything's there
20	L	all you said is a Christian Musical group and the title of the song
21	U	the casting crowns is the musical group
22	U	that's the one
23	L	one moment please
24	U	but the only problem right now is that i cant get a hold of the librarian
25	U	ok
26	U	ok how long do i have to wait [Lib. First Name]?
27	L	I need to look at the catalog
28	U	wat catalog
29	U	?
30	U	oh ok
31	L	the [library name] catalog
32	U	let me know when ur done
33	U	going to request items that the library has
34	U	oh ok take ur time ,no need to rush
35	U	let me know when ur done [Lib. First Name]
36	L	we have other cds by Casting Crowns but not with that song
37	L	Amazonn does have the cd though
38	L	*Amazon as in Amazon.com
39	U	u want to order it
40	U	dont want to order it,if ur tryin to tell me to order it
41	U	i dont want to order it
42	U	it's too expensive
43	L	I am just informing you

44	L	Here is the link to [library name] catalog with the list of cds that is owned by the library:
45	U	wat does imforming u
46	U	mean?
47	U	wat does imforming me mean?
48	U	r u tryin to tell me to buy it from amazon
49	L	[URL sent]
50	U	no thank u,im not going to order it [Lib. First Name]
51	L	just letting you know if you wanted to purchase it that it is on Amazon not telling you to buy it
52	U	so wat does the catalog say abt casting crowns worship cd
53	U	is wat i want to request from the library and i wanna borrow it
54	U	oh ok
55	L	They have other cds with their music
56	U	is there any way tht u can help me
57	U	[Lib. First Name]
58	U	yea
59	L	I already did the best that I could
60	L	It is not at [library name]
61	L	which includes the [branch] libraries in the system
62	U	im not tryin 2 to b rude to u
63	U	im never rude to librarians when i chat wif me
64	U	*when i chat wif them
65	U	rude
66	U	i wouldnt dare to b rude to them
67	U	cuz that's not nice
68	U	im sry am i stressing u out [Lib. First Name]
69	U	im sry
70	U	i didnt mean to stress u out
71	U	miss
72	L	May like to try the [nearby other library name] if you like they may have the copy
73	U	give me the library name
74	U	ill check it out
75	U	i need the name of the library
76	U	hey i got a question to ask u
77	L	[URL sent for other library catalog]
78	U	wat does offsite mean?
79	U	it says it on the catalog
80	U	oh ok

81	L	that the item is at another facility which is not located in [city name]
82	U	tell me wat offsite mean
83	U	i dont get it
84	L	and it must be requested in advance and cannot be taken out of the library
85	U	so it means tht it isnt in the library
86	U	i meant it isnt in [city name]
87	U	it's somewhere else
88	U	no matter wat im going to help myself to borrow the cd
89	U	im not giving up on it
90	L	The request must be made once you have identified which library
91	L	good luck
92	U	so i get to request it once
93	L	{Have a great day and thank you for using [service name]}
94	U	no more than twice?
95	U	request it
96	U	?
97	U	tht wat ur tryin to say
98	U	/
99	U	/
100	U	?
101	U	wait
102	U	not done yet
103	U	[Lib. First Name]
104	U	r u busy?
105	U	have to go?
106	U	[Lib. First Name]?
107	U	if u have to go,ill let u go
108	L	{Have great holiday!}
109	L	ChatLibrarianEnded;.

[**Note from L:** Patron seems a little bit off. Tried to assist but did not seem to grasp the information.]

This transcript reveals a long, somewhat tortured encounter. Ultimately the librarian does answer the user's question, although the answer is in the negative: the library does not have the requested CD for a Christian musical group. The librarian-user relationship is off to a rocky start, perhaps because of insufficient face-work, starting with the omission of a greeting ritual. The librarian starts with "what did they say?" rather than by saying "hello" or offering another personal greeting. The librarian finds other CDs by the group, but not the one requested, and she determines that Amazon has the CD for sale. The user (most likely a young person perhaps in middle school, judging from the spelling and grammatical errors) is not happy with the suggestion to try Amazon, and the encounter slides further towards an unsuccessful outcome. The librarian exhibits patience and professionalism, but fails to make a relational connection to the user, and the comment in line 108 "have a great holiday" seems insincere, although it was probably meant as an attempt to end the encounter on a positive note. The librarian ignores the user's attempt to hang on to the chat conversation in lines 101 to 107, by not responding to the user's question: "r u busy?" In the strict sense, it is successful in the content dimension (the librarian finds that the library does not have the CD and suggests a referral to another nearby library). Also, note that the user struggles with library jargon, such as "offsite" and "the catalog" and does not have the vocabulary needed to understand what "informing" means. The librarian's explanations are terse, and clearly overestimate the user's ability to catch on. The librarian's closing not at the end is "Patron seems a little bit off. Tired to assist but did not seem to grasp the information." This entry from the librarian indicates that he or she realized that the encounter did not go well, but views this as the user's problem, not because of the lack of face-work on the librarian's part.

CONCLUSION

The results of these extensive research activities conclude that a combination of both content (information exchanged, what was said, what was achieved) and relational dimensions (what the conversation said about the relationship of the participants, how the information was received) is important for determining perceptions of satisfaction and success, culminating in the development of the model. When asked to describe successful reference encounters using the critical incident technique, library users, librarians, and VRS nonusers consistently said that a combination of success in both dimensions was critically needed (Flanagan 1954; see also Radford 1996, 2006b; Connaway and Radford 2011). Librarians, as well as users, highly value information delivered/received in addition to interpersonal/relational aspects. Interestingly, a greater proportion of online users were found to value content delivery in VRS more than those in FtF contexts, based on critical incident analyses (Radford 1996, 1999, 2006a). Relational dimensions were revealed to be highly important as well, with librarians being especially sensitive to the user's attitude in perceptions of unsuccessful VRS critical incidents, as was also found to be the case in FtF reference service (Radford 1993, 1999, 2006b). When librarians described unsuccessful encounters, these were most frequently attributed to "bad guy" users who were angry, impatient, rude, or had poor information literacy skills.

Interestingly, focus group interviews and transcript analysis found important differences in communication patterns and information-seeking choices of participants ages twelve through twenty-eight (see Radford and Connaway 2007; Connaway, Radford, Dickey, Williams, and Confer 2008). As shown by the examples from younger users, relational dimensions are especially central to teens and young adults who are undergoing rapid emotional and physical development. These younger library users also value content in the form of information delivery, expecting direct answers and becoming impatient when they perceive that their information needs are not taken seriously. They frequently want "just the facts," and will resist instruction when it is forced upon them. Interestingly, they were more receptive to instruction in FtF reference encounters than they were in VRS modes. However, librarians rated instruction to be of higher quality in VRS when there was a teachable moment. That is, when librarians asked, "do you want to find out more about how I found this information" or "how do I use this resource in the future?" all types of users were more receptive in VRS.

After extensive analysis of VRS live-chat session transcripts, the detailed category scheme of facilitators and barriers first developed by Radford (1999, 2006a) was expanded and refined. Along with the critical incident analysis from the Seeking Synchronicity (Radford and Connaway 2005–2008) and Cyber Synergy (Radford, Connaway, and Shah 2011–2014) surveys and phone interviews, this category scheme formed the framework for the theoretical model and informed the bulleted lists of critical factors for each quadrant. Although the model was derived from reports gathered specifically from reference encounters, it has significant implications and relevance for other instances of professional encounters.

All the examples above illustrate how the theoretical model builds on the relational framework described throughout this book. The model encourages reflective practice and service excellence in all contexts and modes of service delivery, including FtF, virtual, and blended environments. It also emphasizes the importance of a mix of both information and relationship development as being critical for successful reference encounters. As well, it highlights the need for librarians to develop strategies for cultivating excellent interpersonal relationships with users in digital environments to mirror those in FtF reference encounters. One important implication of the work that forms the research basis for the model is the need to consider the sustainability and success of VRS and ongoing relevance of FtF reference. Future success may be contingent upon building positive relationships with all users, including the younger ones. If positive relationships are not formed at early, impressionable ages, individuals may increasingly turn elsewhere (such as search engines and social media sites) to meet their information needs, to the exclusion of libraries.

Let's consider some additional implications of this model for librarians:

- Information and relationship development are both critical to successful interactions.
- Support and sustainability of library services are, to a large extent, dependent upon developing and maintaining positive relationships with VRS and FtF users and attracting potential users.
- Content and technical skills are also vitally important for success.
- Increased focus on interpersonal communication and relational development is important for user satisfaction.
- Emphasis on the user's point of view enables satisfaction and success.
- Convenience of service is key to users.
- Each encounter has a dual goal of providing information/instruction and building positive relationships.

What librarians might find surprising about the model is the importance of the relational, interpersonal aspect in comparison to the content or information aspects. Most master's programs in library and information science focus on teaching reference sources and systems, with the study of interpersonal communication processes given only surface-level attention. The highly technical arena of both FtF and VRS demands that students be educated in methods to find quality information and critically evaluate sources. This work indicates that, yes, content and technical skills are vitally important, but also that relational dimensions are critical and vibrant elements in determining successful reference service from the viewpoints of both librarians and library users. Many individuals, both those new to library environments and experienced professionals, can gain valuable insights from looking at these encounters from a different perspective. This model offers a unique perspective, and provides an increased understanding of reference encounters across FtF and VRS environments. These insights can open avenues for achieving greater success and satisfaction for all involved.

REFERENCES

Connaway, Lynn. S., Dickey, Timothy. J., and Radford, Marie L. 2011. "'If It's Too Inconvenient I'm Not Going After It': Convenience as a Critical Factor in Information-Seeking Behaviors." *Library and Information Science Research* 33 (3): 179–90.

Connaway, Lynn. S. and Marie L. Radford. 2011. *Seeking Synchronicity: Revelations and Recommendations for Virtual Reference.* Dublin, OH: OCLC Research.

Connaway, Lynn. S., Marie. L. Radford, Timothy J. Dickey, Jocelyn D. Williams, and Patrick C. Confer. 2008. "Sense-Making and Synchronicity: Information-Seeking Behaviors of Millennials and Baby Boomers." *Libri* 58: 123–35.

Flanagan, John. C. 1954. "The Critical Incident Technique." *Psychological Bulletin* 5: 327–58.

Goffman, Erving. 1964. "The Neglected Situation." *American Anthropologist* 66: 133–36.

———. 1967. *Interaction Ritual: Essays on Face-to-Face Behavior.* Garden City, NY: Doubleday.

Ito, Mizuko, and Daisuke Okabe. 2006. "Technosocial Situations: Emergent Structuring of Mobile E-mail Use." In *Personal, Portable, Pedestrian: Mobile Phones in Japanese Life,* edited by Mizuko Ito and Daisuke Okabe, 257–276. Cambridge, MA: MIT Press.

Nicol, Erica C., and Linda Crook. 2012. "Now It's Necessary: Virtual Reference Services at Washington State University, Pullman." *Journal of Academic Librarianship* 2 (39): 161–68. doi:101016/jacalib.2012.09.017.

Radford, Marie L. 1993. "Relational Aspects of Reference Interactions: A Qualitative Investigation of the Perceptions of Users and Librarians in the Academic Library." PhD diss., Rutgers, The State University of New Jersey.

———. 1996. "Communication Theory Applied to the Reference Encounter: An Analysis of Critical Incidents." *Library Quarterly* 66 (2): 123–37.

———. 1999. *The Reference Encounter: Interpersonal Communication in the Academic Library.* Chicago: Association of College and Research Libraries.

———. 2006a. "Encountering Virtual Users: A Qualitative Investigation of Interpersonal Communication in Chat Reference." *Journal of the American Society for Information Science and Technology* 57 (8): 1046–059.

———. 2006b. "The Critical Incident Technique and the Qualitative Evaluation of the Connecting Libraries and Schools Project." *Library Trends* 54 (1): 46–64.

Radford, Marie L., and Lynn S. Connaway. 2005–2008. *Seeking Synchronicity: Evaluating Virtual Reference Services from User, Non-User, and Librarian Perspectives.* Dublin, OH: OCLC Research, 2008. www.oclc.org/research/themes/user-studies/synchronicity.html.

———. 2007. "'Screenagers' and Live Chat Reference: Living Up to the Promise." *Scan* 26 (1): 31–39.

———. 2009. "Thriving on Theory: A New Model for Virtual Reference Encounters." In *Proceedings of the 72nd ASIS&T Annual Meeting: Thriving on Diversity—Information Opportunities in a Pluralistic World,* edited by Andrew Grove. November 6–11, 2009. Vancouver: ASIS&T. www.asis.org/Conferences/AM09/proceedings/.

————. 2013. "Not Dead Yet! A Longitudinal Study of Query Type and Ready Reference Accuracy in Live Chat and IM Reference." *Library and Information Science Research* 35 (1): 2–13.

Radford, Marie L., Lynn S. Connaway, and Chirag Shah. 2011–2014. *Cyber Synergy: Seeking Sustainability through Collaboration between Virtual Reference and Social Q&A Sites.* OCLC Research, 2014. www.oclc.org/research/activities/synergy/default.htm.

Rainie, Lee, and Barry Wellman. 2012. *Networked: The New Social Operating System.* Cambridge, MA: MIT Press.

Ross, Catherine S., and Patricia Dewdney. 1998. "Negative Closure: Strategies and Counter-Strategies in the Reference Transaction." *Reference and User Services Quarterly* 38 (2): 151–63.

Ruesch, Jurgen, and Gregory Bateson. 1968. *Communication: The Social Matrix of Psychiatry.* New York: Norton.

Savolainen, Reijo. 2005. "Everyday Life Information Seeking." In *Theories of Information Behavior,* edited by Karen E. Fisher and Lynne McKechnie, 143–48. Medford, NJ: Information Today, Inc.

Spagnolli, Anna, and Luciano Gamberini. 2007. "Interacting via SMS: Practices of Social Closeness and Reciprocation." *British Journal of Social Psychology* 46 (2): 343–64.

Spilioti, Tereza. 2011. "Beyond Genre: Closings and Relational Work in Text-Messaging." In *Digital Discourse: Language in the New Media,* edited by Crispin Thurlow and Kristine Mroczek, 67–85. Oxford, UK: Oxford University Press.

Thurlow, Chrispin, and Michele Poff. 2011. "Text Messaging." In *Handbook of the Pragmatics of CMC,* edited by Susan C. Herring, Dieter Stein, and TuijaVirtanen, Berlin and New York: Mouton de Gruyter.

Walther, Joseph B. 2007. "Selective Self-presentation in Computer-mediated Communication: Hyperpersonal Dimensions of Technology, Language, and Cognition." *Computers in Human Behavior* 23 (5): 2538–57.

Walther, Joseph B., Tracy Loh, and Laura Granka. 2005. "Let Me Count the Ways: The Interchange of Verbal and Nonverbal Cues in Computer-Mediated and Face-to-Face Affinity." *Journal of Language and Social Psychology* 24 (1): 36–65.

Walther, Joseph. B., Brandon V.D. Heide, Stephanie T Tong, Caleb T. Carr and Charles C. Atkin. 2010. "Effects of Interpersonal Goals on Inadvertent Intrapersonal Influence in Computer-Mediated Communication." *Human Communication Research* 36 (3): 323–47.

Watzlawick, Paul, Janet Beavin Bavelas, and Don D. Jackson. 1967. *Pragmatics of Human Communication.* New York: Norton.

NOTES

1. An earlier version of this model was presented at ASIS&T and described in the conference proceedings. The model is presented here with permission of Lynn Silipigni Connaway and OCLC, Inc. See Radford, M. L., and Connaway, L. S. (2009). "Thriving on Theory: A New Model for Virtual Reference Encounters." Paper presented on panel *Opportunities, Threats, and Theoretical Approaches: Research in Traditional and Social Virtual Reference Quality.* ASIS&T 2009 Proceedings of the 72nd ASIS&T Annual Meeting, *Thriving on Diversity—Information Opportunities in a Pluralistic World.* Edited by Andrew Grove. Vol. 46. Conference held in Vancouver, BC, on November 6–11, 2009. [Available at www.asis .org/Conferences/AM09/proceedings/]. The model was also described in a conference paper: Radford, M. L., and Connaway, L. S. (2009). "CREATing a New Theoretical Model for Reference Encounters in Synchronous Face-To-Face and Virtual Environments." Presented at the 2009 ALISE Conference, Denver, CO, January 20–23, 2009.

2. For the most part, reference encounters are discussed in this book as dyads between one librarian and one library user. We do recognize that in many cases there are teams of librarians working together at a service desk or consulted in referrals, and that sometimes users also may be part of a team, as in group work assignments.

Concluding Remarks

What Did We Learn?

There is a mismatch between what people do in unique situations, and what our prevailing beliefs in a transmission theory of communication say they do. Our contemporary understanding of communication is still firmly based in the seventeenth century intellectual framework inspired by John Locke's idealization of philosophical communication, which was concerned with the transmission of clear and distinct ideas. However, as we have seen, Locke knew that such an ideal situation was impossible in practice, and that the transmission of information in the form of messages from one person or place to another is only one aspect of what happens when two people talk to each other in a conversation. In these encounters, we are doing much more than simply transmitting an idea from one mind to another. The act of communicating is an end in itself. It serves to create the social situations in which we form our significant relationships with others. It is the process by which we create, maintain, and protect our face and the face of those with whom we are speaking.

Perhaps the central lesson of this book is that information professionals need to consider the process of interpersonal communication (what is being done) as much as the content (what is being said). In proposing this, we follow the lead of communication scholar James Carey, who wrote:

> The activities we collectively call communication—having conversations, giving instructions, imparting knowledge, sharing significant ideas, seeking information, entertaining and being entertained—are so ordinary and mundane that it is difficult for them to arrest our attention. Moreover, when we intellectually visit this process, we often focus on the trivial and unproblematic, so inured are we to the mysterious and awesome in communication. (Carey 1992, 24)

Our reclaiming of such authors as Ruesch, Bateson, Watzlawick, and Goffman clearly and dramatically reveals that what is said in a conversation is only a very small part of what is going on. We learned that interpersonal communication is always a two-sided process that serves to coordinate the actions of people with one other. It is also the means by which meanings are made and managed (rather than transmitted). We also learned that there is always tension inherent between the two parties involved, because neither party is, or possibly could be, in full control of what is going on at any given moment. Your actions may be dependent on mine, but at the same time, my actions are also dependent on yours.

We learned that, despite what the transmission theory of communication tells us, there is no source or receiver in a conversation. I am not sending messages and you are not receiving them. We do not have discrete and identifiable roles in this process, because both of us are fully involved in what develops. We learned that we must replace the idea of linearity with that of reflexivity—the notion that people are always affected by, as well as producers of, messages.

With respect to the role of interpersonal communication in the professional world, we learned that the transmission view privileges what is spoken about, and emphasizes how this talk can help achieve strategic ends that benefit what the model refers to as "the sender," or the originator of the message. By rejecting this model and by looking at interpersonal communication through a relational and interactional lens, we are able to see that our places of work consist of patterns of conversations. Successful communication is less about promoting and imposing a particular message for others to follow, and more about promoting certain forms of conversation where the relational dimension of communication is recognized as being as, if not more, important than the content dimension. As communicators in professional settings, our role is to be the custodian of the communication process. We need to initiate, sustain, and transform patterns of communication within our workplaces. The librarian in a reference encounter has to be fully aware of and sensitive to the interaction context. She must recognize that the communication act and its meaning are always contingent, and that she must seek to speak in ways that invite further conversation rather than simply persuade the other person to accept what she has to say. We have learned that there are no tips or strategies that will guide us through our conversations such that they will always be successful and always go the way we want them to.

We learned that a single utterance, or movement, or the slightest facial expression can change the meaning or direction of an encounter in a split second, and that the meanings created and taken away from a conversation are always in a state of continual creation. We learned that conversation is not about doing things correctly, but rather about doing things wisely. We learned that what is most important about conversation is recognizing critical moments and then acting wisely on them. We learned that the key element of successful conversations is not the personal characteristics of the participants (i.e., their honesty, integrity, or intelligence), nor the effect of any single particular action that may turn the conversation in ways that the speaker desires. Rather, we learned that communication is a continuing process of action and reflection.

We also discovered that we cannot compare our performance in a conversation against some ideal of what a skilled communicator would do. We can certainly check the boxes in a rubric designed to evaluate our performance in some highly managed role-playing exercise, but we have found that the success of the interaction will always depend on the response to those actions and the subsequent interaction pattern that is created. We learned that communicating wisely is not a matter of behaving according to a previously determined profile, but rather of becoming immersed in unfinished and unfolding patterns of communication in which meaning and significance can change in the most unpredictable ways. We learned that the goal of the wise communicator is to sense and respond appropriately within these patterns as they are happening. The model of the reference encounter presented in this book, therefore, is not a prescription. It does not say that this is how you should go about talking to others in order to have successful interactions by trying to fit your communication behavior to an abstract description. Rather, we are advocating that it is much more important to be responsive to the other people in a social situation than to try and make the situation fit a textbook description. The model points out that to have successful encounters it is necessary to have both positive relationship development and positive content/information dimensions. Every encounter takes place against the backdrop of situation, participant characteristics, and mode of communication. These context elements have enormous impact on whether the participants will feel good about and satisfied with the encounter, or become upset and shamed, or disappointed and unsatisfied.

Our goal has been to provide an intellectual discussion of all the facets of this process within professional contexts, and to reclaim and present rich theory that calls our attention to the ordinary, perhaps overlooked, aspects of everyday communication. We have also illustrated the application of these theoretical frameworks with examples from library contexts, aiming to provide readers with fresh insights to view and understand all that is, to use Carey's words, "mysterious and awesome" about our interpersonal communication encounters.

REFERENCE

Carey, James. "A Cultural Approach to Communication." In *Communication as Culture*, by James Carey, 13–36. New York: Routledge. 1992.

APPENDIX

Physics/Bumper Car Transcript

Line	Participant	Transcript
1	U (User)	Physics
2	L (Librarian)	[Please hold for the next available librarian. If you would like a transcript of this session e-mailed to you, please type your full e-mail address now.]
3	L	[[Name]—A librarian has joined the session.]
4	U	when you drive forward in a bumper car at high speed and then you slam into the car in front of you, you find yourself thrown forward in your car. Which way is ur car accelerating?
5	L	thank you for holding I was working with another patron.
6	L	Is this a homework question.
7	L	I'm not an expert on driving so I really can't answer that.
8	U	can u find a website or something
9	L	I'm not sure what you are asking.
10	U	when you drive forward in a bumper car at high speed and then you slam into the car in front of you, you find yourself thrown forward in your car. Which way is ur car accelerating?
11	U	. . . .
12	U	hello?
13	L	Is this a homework a homework assignment. what subject is it.

14	L	I really don't understand how I can answer that for you.
15	U	can i hav another librarian
16	L	The information you gave you me does not help me find any resources to help you.
17	L	What do you mean by which way is your car accerlaerating. Are you sure thats what your assignment asks.
18	U	Yes
19	L	What subject is this question from?
20	U	Physics
21	L	Okay just one moment.
22	L	[Web Page sent]
23	L	This is one site that may help.
24–25	L	[Pages sent]
26	L	this is another site that youmay try forhelp.
27	L	When we disconnect youwill have these links in a transcript.
28	L	[Page sent]
29	L	This site looks to be very helpful.
30–32	L	[Pages sent]
33	U	this isn't helpful
34	L	Well I really don't have any other resources that can assit you.
35	L	[Page sent]
36	L	I cannot answer the question for you, I don't have the physics knowledge.
37	L	Maybe you will need to ask your instructor for a clear understanding.
38	L	[Page sent]

39	U	do u kno ne1 who does
40	L	[Page sent]
41	L	Sorry I do not.
42	U	ok
43	L	I have a few patron that I ned to assist.
44	U	ok bye
45	L	[Thank you for using [VRS]! If you have any further questions, please contact us again.]

Transcript from Radford, Marie L. and Lynn S. Connaway, L. S. (2005–2008). *Seeking Synchronicity: Evaluating Virtual Reference Services from User, Non-User, and Librarian Perspectives.* Dublin, OH: OCLC Research, 2008. www.oclc.org/research/themes/user-studies/synchronicity.html.

ABOUT THE AUTHORS

MARIE L. RADFORD is professor in the Department of Library and Information Science and director of the PhD Program at Rutgers, the State University of New Jersey's, School of Communication and Information. Previously, she was acting dean of Pratt Institute's School of Information and Library Science and a department head at the Cheng Library at The William Paterson University of New Jersey. She teaches courses in qualitative research methods, library and information science theory, management, and reference services. She gives frequent keynote speeches and webinars, presents research papers at international and national conferences, and publishes widely in prestigious library journals. Marie's recent books include *Research Methods in Library and Information Science, 6th Edition.* with Lynn Silipigni Connaway (Libraries Unlimited, 2017) and *Leading the Reference Renaissance* (Neal-Schuman, 2012). She received the 2010 ALA/RUSA Mudge Award for distinguished contributions to reference service. She holds a PhD in Communication, Information, and Library Studies from Rutgers University and an MSLS from Syracuse University.

GARY P. RADFORD is professor and chair of the Department of Communication Studies at Fairleigh Dickinson University, Madison, New Jersey. The recipient of numerous teaching and research awards, he teaches courses in interpersonal communication, communication theory, and communication philosophy. He serves as editor-in-chief of the *Atlantic Journal of Communication,* and is past chair of the Philosophy and Communication Division of the National Communication Association. Gary is the author of *On the Philosophy of Communication* (Thomson Wadsworth, 2005), *On Eco* (Thomas Wadsworth, 2003), and is coeditor of *Transgressing Discourses: Communication and the Voice of the Other* (SUNY Press, 1997). He holds a PhD in Communication, Information, and Library Studies from Rutgers University and an MS in Speech Communications from Southern Illinois University.

INDEX